QUANTIFICATION
IN PSYCHOLOGY

8-54

BASIC CONCEPTS IN PSYCHOLOGY SERIES

developed at The University of Michigan
Edward L. Walker, Editor

GENERAL

PSYCHOLOGY AS A NATURAL AND SOCIAL SCIENCE	Edward L. Walker
TEACHING THE BEGINNING COURSE IN PSYCHOLOGY	Edward L. Walker and Wilbert J. McKeachie
A LABORATORY MANUAL FOR THE CONTROL AND ANALYSIS OF BEHAVIOR	Harlan L. Lane and Daryl Bem
QUANTIFICATION IN PSYCHOLOGY	William L. Hays
BASIC STATISTICS	**William L. Hays**

PSYCHOLOGY: A NATURAL SCIENCE

NEUROPSYCHOLOGY: THE STUDY OF BRAIN AND BEHAVIOR	Charles M. Butter
SENSORY PROCESSES	Mathew Alpern, Merle Lawrence, and David Wolsk
PERCEPTION	Daniel J. Weintraub and Edward L. Walker
PERCEPTUAL DEMONSTRATION KIT	Daniel J. Weintraub and Edward L. Walker
HUMAN PERFORMANCE	Paul M. Fitts **and Michael I. Posner**
CONDITIONING AND INSTRUMENTAL LEARNING	Edward L. Walker

PSYCHOLOGY: A SOCIAL SCIENCE

MOTIVATION: A STUDY OF ACTION	David Birch and Joseph Veroff
THE CONCEPT OF HUMAN DEVELOPMENT	Elton B. McNeil
PSYCHODYNAMICS: THE SCIENCE OF UNCONSCIOUS MENTAL FORCES	Gerald S. Blum
ASSESSMENT OF HUMAN CHARACTERISTICS	E. Lowell Kelly
COGNITIVE PROCESSES	Melvin Manis
SOCIAL PSYCHOLOGY: AN EXPERIMENTAL APPROACH	Robert B. Zajonc

QUANTIFICATION
IN PSYCHOLOGY

WILLIAM L. HAYS

The University of Michigan

BROOKS/COLE PUBLISHING COMPANY

Belmont, California

A Division of Wadsworth Publishing Company, Inc.

L. C. cat. card No.: 67-12819

Printed in the United States of America

SERIES FOREWORD

Basic Concepts in Psychology was conceived as a series of brief paperback volumes constituting a beginning textbook in psychology. Several unique advantages arise from publishing individual chapters as separate volumes rather than under a single cover. Each book or chapter can be written by an author identified with the subject matter of the area. New chapters can be added, individual chapters can be revised independently, and, possibly, competitive chapters can be provided for controversial areas. Finally, to a degree, an instructor of the beginning course in psychology can choose a particular set of chapters to meet the needs of his students.

Probably the most important impetus for the series came from the fact that a suitable textbook did not exist for the beginning courses in psychology at the University of Michigan—Psychology 100 (Psychology as a Natural Science) and Psychology 101 (Psychology as a Social Science). In addition, no laboratory manual treated both the natural science and social science problems encountered in the first laboratory course, Psychology 110.

For practical rather than ideological reasons, the initial complement of authors comes from the staff of the University of Michigan. Coordination among geographically dispersed authors seems needlessly difficult, and the diversity of points of view in the Department of Psychology at Michigan makes the danger of parochialism quite small.

Each author in the Basic Concepts in Psychology Series has considerable freedom. He has been charged to devote approximately half of his resources to elementary concepts and half to topics of special interest and emphasis. In this way, each volume will reflect the personality and viewpoint of the author while presenting the subject matter usually found in a chapter of an elementary textbook.

INTRODUCTION

This book attempts to introduce the student in psychology to measurement. Although the quantitative treatment of data by the methods of statistics is heavily emphasized from the very beginning of a student's training, the methods for obtaining numerical measurements are not emphasized. A large part of this volume concerns methods for arriving at numerical scores from behavioral data. These methods have been chosen for their simplicity, as well as their applicability to a fairly wide range of content. On the other hand, no attempt has been made to make this coverage exhaustive.

The essential theme running throughout this book is that any measurement procedure must have a definite rationale, based in part on theoretical considerations and in part on actual empirical evidence. It is my belief that the student in psychology must see at a fairly early stage in his career the role that theory plays in measurement. Furthermore, the arbitrary character of much of our measurement activity must be realized. The student using this book is expected to have some familiarity with the classical statistical concepts. Certainly, he should have at least some acquaintance with the theory and use of the normal distribution. I believe, however, that the material presented in the companion volume in this series, *Basic Statistics*, is adequate to let the student understand the basis for the methods used and to make applications of most of these methods.

I wish to express my thanks to Professor E. Lowell Kelly and Professor Robert Hefner for their sympathetic help and advice in the preparation of this manuscript. Thanks are also due to Professor William L. Sawrey, who reviewed the original manuscript. In particular, I am indebted to the Series Editor, Professor Edward L. Walker, and to Miss Diane Herren for help beyond the call of duty.

CONTENTS

MEASUREMENT IN SCIENCE

A hallmark of the slow but steady growth of psychology from a branch of speculative philosophy to a scientific discipline is its increasing concern with quantification. It is generally agreed that science has as its ultimate goal the statement of relationships in precise and easily communicated form. The greatest precision and succinctness of communication is achieved by a numerical or quantitative statement of relationships. That is, certain properties of the things studied by the scientist are measured, or given numerical values; and at their simplest, the general principles or laws of the science are statements about the connection between the numerical value of one phenomenon and that of another. An example in physics is Boyle's Law, which states the relationship between temperature and pressure exerted by an enclosed gas. An example in chemistry is the weight relations in chemical reactions as given by the molecular weights of the compounds involved. Modern physics and chemistry are filled with such highly precise statements of numerical relationships, which summarize and communicate results that can be checked in the laboratory.

Naturally, quantitative principles from physics and chemistry represent some of the most highly developed parts of modern science, and principles of similar exactitude and elegance are not so common in other newer, and less well-developed sciences. Only in modern times have the biological sciences, for example, established quantitative principles that are on a par with those established in chemistry and physics. The behavioral sciences (psychology, as well as economics, sociology, political science, and anthropology) still lag behind even biology in this respect.

However, a given discipline that does not possess a large body of established quantitative laws is not necessarily less "good," or less "scientific," than the physical sciences. Science is, after all, properly thought of as *a method for gaining systematic knowledge,* rather than the finished products of that method. Scientific method consists of the application of careful, controlled observation, under conditions that are public and repeatable, followed by communication and attempts at coordination of results. Any pursuit of knowledge that adheres to the ideal of open, careful, and controlled observation, and attempts to arrive at systematic accounts of what was observed and why, is scientific. It is scientific irrespective of the area studied or the details of the methods used. Systematic dating of cultures by potshards is as scientific as any method used in high-energy physics, although the concerns and methods of scientists working in these two fields are understandably different.

In this volume we will confine our attention to some of the modern attempts to apply scientific principles to the study of the behavior of man and the other animals. In order to study behavior scientifically, one must be able at least to describe the circumstances under which the behavior occurs, to describe the behavior itself, and to communicate these observations economically and accurately to others. As is true for all scientists, the psychologist who studies behavior must be able to measure behavior, and the factors that influence behavior, in some way that permits him to record and communicate the relationships he observes. Furthermore, the procedures for recording and communicating the results of one psychologist's observations must themselves be so specific and well-described that another psychologist could, at least in principle, repeat the observations quite independently and check the results. In some of the older scientific fields we take for granted such procedures, which give precise, succinct, and numerical specifications of the scientist's observations. How to devise similar measurement procedures is still a major problem for psychology and her sister behavioral sciences. The modern psychologist knows that he is only at the frontier of the true application of scientific method to the study of behavior. Nevertheless, modern psychology represents a deliberate and self-conscious attempt to apply scientific techniques of observation and communication to the study of behavior. If behavior is to be studied by the standard techniques of scientific method, then problems of appropriate and precise recording of behaviors and situations—problems of measurement—must be faced.

MEASUREMENT AND HUMAN VALUES

For centuries, while man was already applying careful empirical observations to the world about him and developing the foundations for physics, chemistry, biology, and astronomy, with all of their various branches, the serious study of man *himself* was left largely to the poets, priests, politicians, and philosophers of the world. Man as an ethical and religious being, man as a social animal, man as the object or wielder of power, man's place in the universe—all of these questions have been the subjects of inquiry since the dawn of time. "What and who is man?" the finest intellects of the ages have asked, and their answers still move us by their beauty and their profundity. But these are the answers given by informal observation, by intuition, by speculation, by unaided reason, and by revelation. And there are as many answers to this question as there are askers. These answers move us, indeed, but not because they are true or testable in the wide and concrete sense of a physical law. When we read Aristotle, St. Thomas Aquinas, Machiavelli, or Shakespeare, we may exclaim, "Yes, that is exactly what people are like!" But we do so because the author touches our emotions and our private experience, and not because he draws upon the recorded results of a large body of careful, precise, and controlled observation.

There is great confusion over this point; but perhaps the author can at least make his own position clear: The study of man by the poet and the philosopher has always been and will always be necessary to point out the meanings and the values of human existence and the proper role of man in the scheme of things. A scientist acting *as scientist* does not aspire to answer such questions. Psychology properly is concerned with *how* man behaves—as an organism, as a personality, and as a social being, and not with the ultimate values and goals of human life, important as these may be. Viewed in this way, man is as appropriate an object of scientific study as a physical element, a stone, or a tree. The serious psychologist realizes that by treating man as an object of systematic study he by no means answers questions of the meaning of man's existence or obviates such questions. Questions of *how* and of the *ultimate why* are very different indeed, and the true scientist knows his limitations.

Only in the early nineteenth century was a self-conscious effort made by psychologists to divorce themselves from strictly philosophic concerns and to study human behavior objectively. This separation of humanistic and scientific goals was not easy, however; and even today there are those who fail to see that the scientific study of behavior— the application of scientific method to the mechanisms of behavior and its changes—may be quite different from the concerns of the writer, the artist, or the philosopher. Gradually, as the science of psychology develops into a body of precise and well-substantiated principles, the delineation between these two legitimate though different approaches to man will become sharper. We must not forget that the first scientific physicists were natural philosophers, that the early astronomers were also cosmologists and astrologists, and that the first chemists were alchemists. We should also remember that over the centuries such studies evolved into modern physical science. By the standards of these disciplines, scientific psychology is young indeed.

OBSERVATION AND MEASUREMENT

Granted, then, that the proper concern of psychology is the objective study of behavior, its mechanisms, and its underlying psychological foundations, how does one go about objectifying the behavior under study? The first principle of a scientific study is that *the investigator must describe appropriately and unambiguously and communicate explicitly what he observes.* The psychologist, like any other scientist, is under an obligation to report not only what he observes but also the circumstances and methods by which he made his observations. Only if this is done will the observations be scientific, in the sense that other scientists can repeat the circumstances of the observations (at least in principle) and question, accept, or reject their validity. The report of the conditions under which data were collected, in sufficient detail that these observations may be repeated, is an essential ingredient of the scientific enterprise. Indeed, as we shall see, the specification of the conditions of observation is the first step in the *measurement* of a given phenomenon, such as a behavior.

When one can specify the conditions under which something occurred, the next problem is to specify *what* occurred. This must be done in such a way that any other, sufficiently trained observer will be able to say "Yes, that is what is happening," or "No, that did not occur," when he repeats the procedure. What is required of the original investigator is an explicit statement of the procedure he followed while observing and categorizing events as they occurred.

A *systematic rule of procedure that permits one to identify each possible event that might occur in the given observational situation with one of a set of different categories or symbols is called a measurement operation or measurement rule.* In order to measure something, the observer must follow a procedure by which each observed event can be classified unambiguously into a category represented by a label, a number, or other symbol. The words *operation* and *rule* in the definition given above are not to be taken too literally. Sometimes the measurement operation requires the use of a mechanical device such as a thermometer: application of the thermometer is a standardized mechanism or procedure which, when carried out on a given object, gives a number, its temperature. Sometimes the measurement operation may make use of a physical, though nonmechanical, component or stimulus. An example is the use of the intelligence quotient (IQ). A person in this case is presented with a test. After he has responded and his score is computed, he is assigned a number—his IQ score. In another instance the measurement procedure may be a rule. Thus, a physician may routinely diagnose measles when a child shows red spots, a coated tongue, and elevated temperature, and not-measles otherwise. The point is that the measurement operation is always a standardized way of proceeding, which may or may not involve one or more mechanical devices or stimuli, but which always assigns to the object being measured a category, a number, or some other classifying symbol. The mathematician would say that the measurement operation is a standardized rule that maps each of a set of objects into one, and only one, of a set of categories or numbers. Any measurement procedure worthy of the name must have such a well-specified operation or rule, which can be communicated and applied by any sufficiently trained person.

It is possible for the scientist himself to be part of the rule. The chemist, for example, wishes to see whether a certain solution is an acid or a base. Therefore, he inserts a piece of litmus paper into his test tube. If the paper turns pink he classifies the solution as "acid," if blue, as "base." Notice that *both* the chemist and the litmus paper actually enter into this measurement operation. The paper changes its physical composition; but the chemist must say how he perceives its new color before he classifies the solution. To see how the chemist himself might affect the measurement outcome, imagine a color-blind chemist. He might conceivably classify the solution differently from a colleague with normal color vision, even though each sees exactly the same litmus paper. Particularly in psychology the observer or scientist himself is a very important piece of equipment in the measurement operation. In some instances he alone is the entire measurement operation. Consider, for example, a psychiatrist or psychologist who is judging whether a patient is psychotic. The standard procedure is for the diagnostician to take note of all the relevant information about the patient and produce a diagnosis of psychotic or nonpsychotic. His years of training and experience have presumably made him sensitive to the presence or absence of psychosis in a patient. He serves as a measuring device in this instance, just as a thermometer serves as a measuring device for temperature. However, we expect thermometers similarly constructed and calibrated to give the same reading when they are applied in the same way to the same object, and we have every right to expect two similarly trained judges to agree in their diagnosis of a patient. Unfortunately, human measuring devices do not always agree, even when they are similarly trained and have access to precisely the same information. Is the application of such a human instrument then a measurement operation for this situation? Yes, but with the strong qualification that one may have to speak of the measurement of the presence or absence of psychosis according to Doctor A and the measurement according to Doctor B; if they do not agree, they cannot really be thought of as identical measurement devices.

The human component in a measurement operation is almost always present in an investigation. After all, someone has to read the thermometer, score the intelligence test, look at the litmus paper, or read the pressure gauge. Ideally, however, only very negligible fluctuations should occur when measurements of the same objects are made by different observers. Such measurement operations in the physical sciences usually are highly specific and routine. And, as we shall see, many, though not all, psychological measurement operations are also quite specific and routine.

So far, then, we have seen that measurement involves (1) an object of measurement, (2) a specified standard situation, (3) a measurement operation in which a rule of procedure is followed, and (4) an assignment of the object in question to a category, number, or symbolic class. An essential requirement of a measurement operation is that it must enable one to say exactly *how* the category, number or symbol assigned to an object was actually found. The measurement operation must be specifiable.

CATEGORICAL MEASUREMENT

Ordinarily, we think of measurement as the assignment of a *number* to an object, as when weight is measured in pounds, when length is measured in inches, or when a test is scored by the number of questions answered correctly. However, no one would be satisfied with a measurement procedure that simply gave numbers if these numbers had no meaning. For instance, if someone drew a card from a playing deck and assigned *you* the number of the card drawn, would the number mean anything? Would it tell anything about *you?* Note that this procedure could be elaborated into a perfectly good measurement *operation* under certain circumstances. The trouble is that the numbers obtained mean absolutely nothing. At least they mean nothing as applied to the person to whom they are assigned. Thus, the two questions that must be raised next: What roles do numbers play in measurement? How does one discuss the meaning of the results of a measurement operation?

As has already been pointed out, before a scientist can record and communicate the *different* events he observes, he must have some scheme for grouping differing events into different categories or types. At the very least he must have some *classification scheme.* The measurement rule tells him how to go about putting each event into the proper category of his scheme. In everyday life we classify constantly. For example, the common and proper nouns in our language form a large and complex classifying scheme. When we wish to record and communicate what we experience, we place our experience into a particular category by giving it a name. Our training in the language has taught us this measurement procedure. Its formal rules are given in dictionaries and lexicons, which tell us when a particular object of our experience should be called a "teapot" and when an "elephant." Science, too, has its own vocabularies or schemes of categories and labels for the things it studies. In biology, for instance, objects of study are classified as plant and animal. Elaborate rules have been evolved so that any living object can be classified as one or the other with high consensus among biologists. Modern physics has classified elementary particles of matter into such categories as proton, neutron, electron, and positron. The measurement operation for the classification of a particular occurrence of a particle includes, among other things, its observed path on a photographic plate or in a bubble chamber. Medical diagnosis uses a classification scheme that is based partly on the history and symptoms the patient shows and partly on the apparent source of the disease. The skilled diagnostician knows the conventional measurement rules and applies them when he assigns a particular patient to a particular category. All branches of science, in fact, make use of sets of qualitative labels or categories, along with the measurement rules or operations specifying how to assign an observed phenomenon to a given category.

The assignment of objects of observation to categories according to some classifying scheme and following some specified rules of procedure is measurement at its simplest and most primitive level. In psychology this has come to be called *categorical* or *nominal measurement*. When a scheme of classification requires that each observation must go into only one category of a set of categories and that every observation must go into some category, the set of categories is called a *nominal scale*. The categories making up a nominal scale are said to be *mutually exclusive* (each observation must be placed into only one category) and *exhaustive* (every observation must be placed into some category). Furthermore, taken collectively, the categories making up a nominal scale are called an *attribute*. Thus, for mammals the attribute sex has only two categories: male and female. In common usage the attribute hair color for humans has a number of categories, such as blonde, red, brown, white, and so on.

Where does the scientist get his classifying scheme? Such a scheme may come from any number of sources; but usually it is based on (1) theoretical considerations, (2) observed similarities or differences in the appearance or the behaviors of the things studied, and (3) practical considerations. Actually, classification schemes used in the sciences seem to have grown out of a combination of all three sources. Thus, classification of elementary particles by physicists rests on an elaborate theory of atomic structure and on predictions about the relative mass, velocity, and the life of such particles. With such a classification scheme it is possible to identify particles in a laboratory by their tracks or other indicators. On the other hand, the great periodic table used by chemists to classify the elements was developed from the observation that particular substances tend to give similar chemical reactions. The underlying theory of the chemical reactions of substances appears to have grown out of the classification scheme, rather than vice versa. The familiar classification schemes of descriptive biology, such as phyla, genera, and species, grew out of observed structural similarities between animals or plants and the observation that only particular kinds of organisms can interbreed. On the other hand, this classification scheme stimulated and was completed by theories advanced in such works as Darwin's *On the Origin of Species*. A scheme such as the familiar classification of workers into white-collar and blue-collar categories was originally devised to provide a useful and descriptive distinction between two groups of people. The distinction the investigators made happened to be related to still other things they were attempting to predict.

Any workable classifying scheme must of necessity omit some information about the things being classified. Any phenomenon or event the scientist observes will have many distinguishable attributes or characteristics; but the scientist must first single out the property or properties relevant to the question under study. For example, when the biologist classifies winged insects into orders such as Lepidoptera or Dioptera, he pays particular attention to the bodily structure and life cycle of the particular insect. He ignores such prominent features as the color of their wings. When a physician measures the blood pressure of a patient, he pays attention to the fluctuations reflected on the dial of the measuring instrument. He is not influenced by such a thing as the patient's income. When a psychologist gives a student an intelligence test, he bases the score purely on the performance shown on the test and not on other, obvious features of the student, such as his hair color. The scientist ignores a great many properties of the object being measured when those properties are considered irrelevant to the measurement of the characteristic under study. The discrimination of objects into different categories or numerical values is based only on a very small portion of the potential information available about each. The act of measurement necessarily requires that some *abstraction* be made from the complex of characteristics shown by any given event. It is because measurement and processing of data actually do involve abstraction that the scientist is able to record and communicate in concise and precise form. If the scientist tried to record and report everything that might be known about a given event, he could write volumes about each. All of the information might then be made available; but the relevant and significant aspects the scientist wishes to study would be lost in a mass of detail.

NUMERICAL MEASUREMENT

Although any measurement operation can be thought of as involving a set of mutually exclusive and exhaustive categories into which objects of observation are assigned, "measurement" commonly means the assignment of a number to each object measured. For this reason one must inquire into the kinds of numbers that are frequently the end products of measurement operations.

In the first place, numbers may be used simply as arbitrary *names* for the categories into which objects are mapped. In recent years the United States has been divided into service areas, and each has been given a number by the telephone company. These are the familiar area-code numbers. Thus, any telephone subscriber in the New York City area currently is given the number 212, in the Chicago area the number 312, and so forth. The rule for this assignment is provided by a table in the front portion of a telephone directory. If one wishes to know the area code number for a person living in Oshkosh, Nebraska, for example, he simply consults the table. Note that these numbers are only names or arbitrary symbols to denote residence in a particular area. No one would assert that because person X living in Chicago has area code 312 and person Y living in New York has area code 212, that X somehow has 100 units more of something than does person Y. One must always remember that numbers *can* serve merely as names or category labels. Such labels represent *qualitative* differences though not necessarily quantitative differences.

On the other hand, some measurement operations produce *ordinal numbers*. Such numbers simply show the *place in order,* according to some characteristic, each object achieved under observation. For example, in a footrace the runner who breaks the tape is given first place or is assigned the number 1. The runner who comes in second is assigned the number 2, and so on for the other runners. Thus, the race itself can be thought of as a procedure for measuring the speed of each runner according to an earned *ordinal* position. It really makes no difference whether X beats Y by .001 second or by 100 seconds. X is still assigned the number 1 (or first place) and Y the number 2 (or second place) if the relative position of each runner at the finish is all that counts. Ordinal numbers always have the characteristic that they symbolize *relative position* or *relative amount* according to some characteristic. However, *differences in ordinal numbers do not necessarily tell anything at all about the differences in amount of the characteristic the objects actually possess.* Thus, although X comes in first in the race, Y second, and Z third and although $2 - 1 = 1$ and $3 - 2 = 1$ in arithmetic, one cannot say that the difference in speed between Y and Z is the same as the difference in speed between X and Y. From ordinal information alone, all one can say is that X was faster than either Y or Z and that Y was faster than Z in the particular race. A very large variety of measurement operations in psychology yield ordinal numbers. They show only that X was *more something* than Y, and give no information at all about the true amount or quantity of difference between X and Y.

When the measurement operation produces ordinal numbers, it is called *ordinal scaling*. The set of numbers or positions to which a collection of objects may be assigned is called an *ordinal scale*. One very common variety of ordinal scale consists of *ordered categories*. Here, according to some rule, each object is assigned to a category. Moreover, the categories are *themselves* thought of as ordered according to some characteristic. Perhaps the most familiar example of ordered categories is the grading scheme commonly used in schools. A is the highest or best category, B the next highest, C the next, D the next, and E the lowest of all. In principle, all of a group of students might be assigned an A according to some standardized procedure or rule, such as an examination. Similarly, all might be assigned an E. But whatever the distribution of students among categories might be, a student getting an A is supposed to be better than a student getting a B, C, D, or E; a student getting a B is better than one getting a C, D, or E. Here, no information is given about *how much* better an A is than a B or how two A students might differ. Students falling into the same category are treated as having equivalent amounts of the characteristic being measured. Those falling into different categories are thought of as being different in the order given by the categories.

Notice that in this last example the *letters* A, B, C, D, and E were used. This is a conventional alphabetic system of ordering. The ordinal numbers 1st, 2nd, 3rd, 4th, 5th, or other sets of symbols or numbers such as 150, 160, 190, 500, 501, or Monday, Tuesday, Wednesday, Thursday, Friday could also have been used. *For ordinal scaling it is usually immaterial whether sets of numbers or other symbols are used. It is equally immaterial what the particular set of numbers employed actually is, as long as the order of the numbers or symbols parallels the order or amount of the characteristic that objects assigned those numbers or symbols are supposed to show.*

Particularly in the physical sciences, certain measurement operations give numbers for which not only the order but also the arithmetic differences between numbers are meaningful. This is called *interval scaling*. The thermometer is used as a mechanical part of a procedure for assigning a number, temperature, to any given object. Two objects measured with a Fahrenheit thermometer may give readings of perhaps 98° and 112°. Here one can say not only that the second object shows a higher temperature than the first but also that the second object has $112° - 98° = 14°$ *more* temperature than the first. The differences between numerical values can be interpreted directly as differences in amount of the characteristic measured. In interval scaling, when two pairs of numbers differ by the same arithmetic amount, one can be certain that the objects assigned those numbers differ by the same true amount of the characteristic measured. Furthermore, in interval scaling, the numbers assigned to objects may be multiplied by any positive constant number and have any constant number added to them and the result will still be an interval scale (though with a different unit and zero point from the original). This principle is illustrated by the Fahrenheit and Centigrade thermometers. Temperature read on a Centigrade thermometer can always be transformed into Fahrenheit temperature, and vice versa, by multiplying by the appropriate constant and adding a constant. (Fahrenheit temperature $= 9/5$ Centigrade $+ 32$.)

Suppose, for example, there are three objects, X, Y, and Z, and that their measurements on a Fahrenheit thermometer are symbolized by $F(X)$, $F(Y)$, and $F(Z)$. Their measurements on a Centigrade thermometer would be symbolized by $C(X)$, $C(Y)$, and $C(Z)$. If one expressed the ratio of differences in temperature among these objects as

$$\frac{F(X) - F(Y)}{F(X) - F(Z)},$$

one would find exactly the same ratio by stating the differences as

$$\frac{C(X) - C(Y)}{C(X) - C(Z)}.$$

Interval scales always have this property. Ratios of differences between values remain invariant when each value is multiplied by a positive constant or when a constant value is added to each. In an interval scale, both the order of the numbers and the differences between the numbers are significant. The only arbitrary features of interval-scale measurement are the value one chooses to call 0 and the unit of measurement.

Certain physical measurement operations also produce *ratio scales*. The measurement of length is a good example. When object X has a length of 25 feet and object Y a length of 50 feet, it is meaningful to say not only that Y is 25 feet longer than X but also that Y has *twice as much length* as X. Note that this statement is not meaningful when applied to two objects showing temperatures of 25° and 50° Fahrenheit. One does not say that the second object has twice as much temperature as the first. Notice also that the readings of temperature of these same objects taken on a Centigrade thermometer would give a different ratio. In ratio-scale measurement, ratios of values are *directly* interpretable as ratios of amounts of the property being measured. An object with no length at all must get the value 0 length. There is nothing arbitrary about the phenomenon assigned value 0 in a ratio scale—unlike the situation of temperature measurement, in which one can have negative values and the assignment of 0 can be changed about at will. Only the unit of measurement for length is arbitrary. One can quite arbitrarily convert feet into inches, into miles, into meters, or into other units by multiplying by the proper positive constants. Any ratio scale, such as that for length, can be altered by multiplication by a positive constant, and the resulting numbers will still be a ratio scale.

This characteristic of ratio scales implies that different measurement procedures will produce numbers with different interpretations in amount. One cannot, however, treat numbers produced by different varieties of measurement procedures as completely equivalent. *Ordinal numbers* are very different from the *cardinal numbers* provided by interval and ratio scaling. And both ordinal and cardinal numbers are different from *labeling numbers* that are sometimes the result of simple classifying schemes or nominal scaling. Although exactly the same number symbols may be used to express the results of nominal, ordinal, interval, or ratio scaling procedures, the meaning one assigns to the numerical symbols may be very different, depending on the procedures employed. The interpretation of the numbers, according to what each expresses about the *amount* of some property possessed by an object of measurement, depends on the theory and empirical knowledge that actually underlie the measurement operation.

Different measurement operations in psychology are based on a wide variety of theoretical and empirical underpinnings. Some measurement operations yield, at best, only nominal or categorical measurement. Often measurement in psychology is based only on the most informal and ad hoc rules of procedure. On the other hand, rather elaborate theoretical justification exists for some of the operations used by psychologists to measure psychological events. Such theoretically supported procedures can often be regarded as yielding at least interval-scale values to the objects measured. However, before the psychologist can claim that the properties he measures are indeed represented at the interval-scale level—so that differences between numerical values can be interpreted as differences in amount of the property under study—he *must* be able to provide both a theoretical and an empirical justification for his procedure. For a science as undeveloped as psychology in many of its branches, this is not always possible, of course.

But unless such a rationale is available, one has a right to question any interpretation of numerical measurements that treats the numbers as more than labels or as indicators of order. On the other hand, even such labeling numbers or ordinal numbers can be very useful to the scientist in his search for valid and predictive relationships, even though such numbers may not give the scientist the ability to state and to use the relationships he finds as precisely and simply as he would be able to do if the numbers were more adequate reflections of amount.

The basic approach to measurement is the same in the physical, the biological, and the behavioral sciences. A measurement operation is formulated, which takes some aspect of the objects to be studied and abstracts it from all of the other irrelevant characteristics that the object may show. Routine application of this measurement operation then provides at least a categorization or classification for each object under study. Sometimes the measurement operation provides an interval scale number for each object; number differences can be interpreted to reflect the differences that exist among objects according to amounts of the characteristic under study. Some measurement operations consist mainly of the application of a standard measuring instrument, such as a ruler, a thermometer, a galvanometer, or a standardized test. Still others require the participation of the scientist himself as a component of the measurement operation. Some measurement operations require only passive participation of the object being measured. In others a situation must be created in which the object of measurement responds or otherwise behaves. Nevertheless, all measurement operations are ways of arriving at standardized, economical, public, and repeatable descriptions of phenomena, objects, or behaviors.

How does one go about measuring some property of an animal or human? Where does one start? Clearly the psychologist must have some idea of the characteristic he wishes to measure. Even before he faces the problem of how to measure, he must have singled out the property or properties that he feels it important to observe in order to answer his particular research question. Granted that this decision has been made, and he knows that he wants to measure the degree of some property that each of a group of human beings shows, he then must face the question of how to proceed. How will this property be reflected in his observations? What relation exists between the behaviors he can actually observe and the amounts of the property in question? Perhaps this is a property that can be observed directly, and perhaps the individuals to be measured can even be compared directly with a standard. For example, if the scientist wishes to describe the weight of each of a group of boys, his problem is relatively simple. Very routine procedures exist for comparing each boy with a set of standard weights and arriving at a "weight number" for each. On the other hand, suppose that the scientist is interested in the mechanical ability each boy possesses. Here, the problem is more complex, since mechanical ability is hardly a directly observable physical property, and there is no simple standard against which he can judge each boy. Ordinarily, the psychologist would then use a test or a situation designed to elicit evidence of mechanical ability from each subject. Each boy is made to behave in a way that should give evidence of mechanical ability. Then the psychologist has some overt behaviors which can be compared from boy to boy, so that at least some relative standing on this characteristic may be assigned to each subject.

Suppose, however, that the psychologist is interested in a characteristic such as the masculinity of each boy. This is a much more difficult characteristic to define or to elicit as behavior. Certainly there is no obvious standard against which each boy might be compared to measure his degree of this characteristic. The degree of masculinity would probably have to be inferred indirectly from a variety of behavioral responses. Many of the behavioral or physical indicators the psychologist would eventually use in arriving at an index of masculinity might have little or no obvious connection with the trait he hopes to measure. Rather, the psychologist must construct his own measurement operation. It would be based on theory or other empirical studies about the connections, often quite indirect, between responses to situations and masculinity. The measurement of the trait itself may not be at all possible in any direct and obvious way. This raises a point that it is important to bear in mind in any discussion of measurement and, in particular, of the differences in measurement procedures among the various sciences.

FUNDAMENTAL AND DERIVED MEASUREMENT OPERATIONS

In the physical world there are a few properties of objects that are so obvious and all-pervasive in our experience that they were long ago singled out as "fundamental" physical characteristics. One such property is *length,* or *linear extent,* which—as height, breadth, distance, etc.—can be applied to an enormous number of the objects of our experience. Length is a property that almost all objects of our experience possess to some degree. Weight is another very compelling physical property of objects: we think of virtually everything in the field of our everyday experience as having weight. Furthermore, both length and weight can be measured directly by comparisons with standards. We can express the length of an object by comparing it with the length of a standard object such as a ruler. We can determine the weight of an object by achieving a state of balance between it and one or more objects of standard weight. Such measurement operations, in which an amount of the property possessed by an object is determined by a simple and direct comparison with an object showing a standard amount of that property, are called *fundamental measurement operations*. The characteristics of objects that are measurable by fundamental operations are often called *extensive* properties. One need not define length by reference to other quantities. Length is measured *in terms of length*. Similarly, weight is measured in terms of other weights and the principle of a balance. In this sense these properties are truly fundamental.

On the other hand, as the physical sciences developed, scientists turned their attention to other and less obvious properties of objects, which could not be measured by a simple comparison of objects with standards. Rather, the operations for measuring these other, *intensive*, properties had to be *derived* from the known or presumed connections between amounts of the intensive property and amounts of one of the more fundamental characteristics. As an example of such *derived measurement* consider temperature measurement once again. The temperature of an object is not measured by the direct comparison of an object with another object of standard temperature. Instead, the known relationship of increasing temperature to the increasing volume of a fluid in a tube is used. The warmer an object is, the higher will the mercury in an adjacent thermometer rise. What one actually observes when he reads a thermometer is *not* the temperature. It is the height (i.e., cylindrical volume calibrated as length) of a column of mercury. The relationship of this height of the column of mercury to the temperature of the object is derived from what we know about heat and expansion. This known relationship gives us the ability to talk about the height of the column of mercury as though it stood directly for amount of temperature. In this way temperature measurement via thermometer is derived rather than fundamental. Similarly, measurement of air pressure via an aneroid barometer is based on the known connection between increased pressure and the decreased volume of an empty flexible container. The more the container is depressed by the air pressure the farther a pointer moves on a dial to give a reading in distance from some comparison point. We do not see or experience the air pressure directly. We infer it from the distance reading on the dial. Thus, air-pressure measurement is an example of derived rather than fundamental measurement. Still other examples from the physical sciences can be produced to show even more remote and complicated relationships that are used to produce derived measurements. Indeed, some of the most basic and useful concepts of modern physics, such as mass, energy, velocity, and voltage, are examples of properties that are ordinarily measured by derived rather than by fundamental operations. The physical scientist is now at the point where so many relationships among physical properties are known that theories and experimental results can be organized around a few convenient and central characteristic (such as mass, length, and time), and other properties of objects or events can then be deduced. The physical scientist really need not to be concerned by the fact that when he measures the velocity of a star by its spectral shift he uses a derived measurement of a fairly intricate character. All of the necessary theory and experiment has long since been carried out to make this a perfectly reasonable way to measure the star's velocity. Note, however, that what the scientist *really* studies is how far certain lines in a spectrograph appear to be shifted away from a standard, and only by inferences supported by theory and evidence does his observation have anything to do with velocity.

The situation of the psychologist is identical to that of the physical scientist so long as he deals with the physical aspects of his subjects or with the physical characteristics of their behaviors. As physical objects, humans or animals can be measured in physical ways. Behaviors can be measured in the same ways that any other observable physical events can be measured. For many of the psychologists' purposes such measurements are sufficient. On the other hand, the psychologist often wishes to go beyond directly observable behaviors and to measure psychological states or characteristics, which can be inferred only indirectly from observable behaviors. Then, like the physical scientist, he must depend upon measurement operations that are derived from known or theorized connections between the psychological situation of the subject and his behaviors in a given stimulus situation.

The psychologist's task would be simplified if he were content to relate only observables to observables, behaviors to physical stimuli, or concrete behaviors to behaviors and not to concern himself with the underlying psychological conditions those behaviors presumably represent. Indeed, for many years an influential school of thought in American psychology held that this is exactly what psychological research properly *should* do. The measurement problem would not be completely avoided by such an approach, since behaviors and stimuli would still have to be categorized or quantified before relations among them could be stated with clarity and precision. Even so, many such behaviors or stimuli could be treated in purely physical terms. Such an approach would avoid the difficulty of having to infer *underlying* psychological events from behaviors and, thus, avoid the problem of measuring such implicit properties in derived ways. On the other hand, the main current of psychological research has always returned from the study of purely behavioral relationships to the effort to measure nonobservable psychological characteristics and events. The problem of derived measurement is thus continually encountered in psychological research.

MEASUREMENT AND ARITHMETIC

In the case of a fundamental measurement of a property such as length each arithmetic operation on numbers is paralleled by the possibility of a physical operation in terms of length. For example, the addition of numerical length A to numerical length B is paralleled by the physical operation of placing two straight rods end to end, one with length A and the other with length B. When the ends of the two rods are joined, the result is a single rod with $A + B$ amount of length. Thus, the mathematical operation of addition of the two numbers, A and B, is an exact parallel of the *physical addition,* or concatenation, of two amounts of the property being measured. Similarly, laying ten rods of standard length A in series end to end produces a rod with length $10\,A$ just as arithmetically as A multiplied by the number 10 yields the number $10\,A$. If a rod of length A is sawed into three rods of equal length, each will be found to have length $A/3$ just as the rules of arithmetic lead us to expect.

Such physical parallels to the operations of arithmetic can be found quite easily for fundamental properties such as length, weight, or volume. This ability to find parallels to arithmetic operations permits the scientist to perform the purely symbolic and mechanical operations of mathematics and to deduce the results of the parallel physical operations. He does not have actually to put a rod 5 feet long at one end of a rod 2 feet long to discover that their combined length is 7 feet. Each time this problem arises, he knows that the arithmetical result $5 + 2 = 7$ is sufficient to tell him what the result of the physical procedure will be. Derived measurement procedures in the physical sciences depend on known relationships to fundamental properties. Application of mathematics to such derived measurement numbers is justified, ultimately, by the parallel mathematical and physical operations on the fundamental properties. A very important branch of mathematical physics, dimensional analysis, deals with the relations of derived quantities to basic fundamental properties. Dimensional analysis is also concerned with the mathematical requirements that are met by measurements of the various derived properties, such as density, force, power, and current, in terms of more fundamental properties, such as length, mass, and time.

As yet, the social and behavioral sciences lack clear agreement about those properties of man and his behavior that might be identified as fundamental *psychological* properties. Thus, for psychological measurement there exists no clearcut parallel between such mathematical operations as addition and experimental psychological procedures What exactly should one mean by psychological or behavioral addition? This problem may be solved some day; but at the present time only very primitive attempts have been made. It is safe to say that until the day comes and until psychologists and other behavioral scientists isolate and agree upon the fundamental measurement operations from which other measurement procedures will be derived and justified, the theory of measurement of psychological entities will be more incomplete and disorganized than measurement theory in the physical sciences.

PSYCHOLOGICAL AND PHYSICAL MEASUREMENT

It was discovered long ago that the really obvious physical properties of a person or his behavior need have little or nothing to do with psychological properties such as intelligence, or the amount of fear a person is experiencing at a given moment, or what he perceives some stimulus to be. Certainly there seem to be no fundamental or extensive psychological properties that one may measure by simple ruler-like comparisons with a standard, as is possible in the physical sciences. It is true that certain behaviors, like simple choice responses, can be merely counted, whereas other activities of the living organism, such as galvanic skin response, heartbeat, and blood pressure, can be given quite precise physical representation. However, no easily quantified physical aspect of a living being has yet been found sufficiently useful to serve as a fundamental yardstick for searching out psychological relationships. Since psychologists and other behavioral scientists are not at all in agreement about what aspects of psychological life they should identify as the most basic, they cannot be expected to agree on a basic set of properties that ought to be measured in order to provide a standard from which other, derived, measurement operations might be established.

A great many measurement operations in psychology are derived from theoretical postulates. The postulates show how magnitudes of some psychological property *ought* to be reflected in occurrences of particular behaviors. In a great many instances, however, these theoretical rationalizations for measuring in a particular way remain purely theoretical since they are not yet supported by a solid experimental underpinning. It is, of course, quite true that some physical measurement operations appeal ultimately to theory—theory that has not been, or that cannot be, verified. On the other hand, virtually all of the measurement procedures used in the physical sciences rest both on theory, and on a great deal of supporting empirical evidence. This evidence shows not only that the assumed physical relationships on which the measurement procedure rests are tenable but also that the derived measurements are *predictively valid* and actually do the work they were designed to do by giving useful relationships in their own right. Although psychologists and other behavioral scientists are aware of the need to establish the *validity* of a particular measurement operation, in most instances they do not have enough evidence either to support the theoretical foundations of the procedure or to establish its predictive usefulness.

The foregoing should not be taken to mean that the problems of psychological measurement are somehow essentially different from measurement problems in the physical sciences. Neither does it mean that psychologists have been remiss in their responsibility to support their measurement operations with theoretical and empirical backing. On the contrary, psychologists are acutely aware of the difficulty of this problem and give a great deal of effort and attention to the establishment of theoretically and empirically valid measurement operations. The problem is exceedingly complex, however, and it is unfair to compare the accomplishments of only a few generations of psychologists with the accomplishments of a line of physical scientists that extends into the distant past. Much remains to be done, and it is significant that research into problems of measurement occupies a great deal of the attention of psychologists today.

Humans and other animals behave in the presence of stimuli. They also have implicit psychological characteristics, abilities, wants, emotions, habits, attitudes, and perceptions, which are not directly observable but which must clearly lie behind their behaviors. In order to measure these psychological characteristics, one must infer their presence and their degree from behavior. Theory and external evidence supply a connection that permits one to infer and, hence, to measure an unobservable psychological situation by means of an observable behavioral event. In some areas of study appropriate theories and funds of evidence exist. In these areas measurement operations can be constructed on a firm base. In others, psychologists have not yet agreed on how some psychological property or event is to be measured. And yet, the psychologist's situation it not really different from that of the chemist, trying to establish an atomic weight for an element. Here, too, is an implicit, not directly observable property. The atomic weight can be inferred only from the way in which the element behaves in standardized situations. Theory provides the essential link between the experimental behavior of the element and the assignment of an atomic weight to it. That the measurement operation is valid is ultimately shown by the predictions one can make of still other behaviors of the particular element. The possibility of such predictions in turn adds strength to the theory of atomic structure. Psychologists have much the same goal. By their attempts to measure, they not only refine their ability to describe and communicate behavior, but also refine the theoretical underpinning on which such measuremen operations depend. Validation of measurement operations by predictions of still other behaviors serves simultaneously to support the theoretical base.

The following section deals with a few simple examples of measurement operations employed in psychology. These examples show the role a specific theoretical position and a set of empirical evidence play in the creation of a measurement operation. Operations based on direct physical or physiological measurement, although very important in psychological research, are not dealt with. And we shall not be discussing topics such as psychogalvanic skin response, heartrate indicators, or electroencephalograms or any of the hundreds of other physical or physiological techniques that psychologists have found useful. Rather, the discussion is confined to methods for measuring psychological magnitudes from the behaviors of one or more subjects toward one or more stimuli. The reason for this choice is simple: It is to emphasize the role theoretical assumptions play in dictating the form a psychological measurement technique takes. By and large, the procedures discussed are truly *quantitative*, being ones that often provide numerical measurements at the interval scale level. In addition, the psychological properties with which this text is concerned are implicit. They are properties that cannot be directly or simply related to observable behaviors. All the techniques discussed have certain statistical features. And it is necessary that the student have competence in the rudiments of statistics. The required statistical materials are presented in another volume of this series, *Basic Statistics*.

EXERCISES AND PROBLEMS

1. Explain why numerical measurement permits the scientist to communicate relationships in their most economical form.
2. Why must scientific communication necessarily leave out some of the detail of ordinary experience?
3. What is meant by the term "measurement operation"?
4. Why is *communication* one of the chief goals of the scientist?
5. Imagine, if you can, the most refined measurement process now known to man. To what extent is the human component ruled out of this measurement process?
6. From your experience with courses in the natural sciences, give an example of measurement at the categorical level. (Do not use examples given in this text.)
7. Attack this proposition: "Any measurement scheme involves some

degree of abstraction." Cite examples from the sciences showing that this is not the case.

8. Give an example, from the sciences or from everyday life, that illustrates ordinal measurement.

9. Give an example of numerical measurement in which the numbers have no meaning other than at the (a) ordinal level, and (b) at the categorical level.

10. Give an example from everyday life of measurement at the ordinal level, which is frequently treated as measurement at some higher level.

11. Show how ordinal measures can be translated into any set of ordered symbols without loss of meaning.

12. Give an example of interval scaling. (Do not use ones given in the text.) Remember, there must be a well-defined unit of measurement; but the definition of zero must be flexible.

13. Is there an example of ratio scaling not cited in the text? When one deals with logarithms of numbers, what level of scaling is supposed?

14. In order to compare a pair of college football teams, a sports writer simply computed the average number taken from the jerseys of the starting eleven for each team. He found that team A had a higher average number than team B. He therefore concluded that team A must be superior to team B. What objections can be raised to the procedure of averaging such football numerals? What objections can be raised to the sports writer's conclusion?

15. Give an example of a psychological characteristic which might be of interest to measure, but of which there is no direct means of measurement.

16. State, in simple language, the difference between fundamental and derived measurement. Give an illustration of each.

17. Give an example of a psychological characteristic that can be measured directly in physical terms. Argue that the psychologist need make no inference in going from the physical measurement to the psychological state in which he is ultimately interested.

18. An educator simply averaged the grade points received by students in different courses. If a grade-point average is a reflection of academic ability, what is wrong with this procedure?

19. Why is a theory that links stimulus to response of particular importance in psychological measurement?

20. Why should results of specific measurement techniques differ from one another, depending on the theoretical assumptions on which each were based, even when they utilize the same behavior?

The essential problem of quantitative measurement in psycholog is that of inferring numerical values from behavior. Measurement of physical property of a person or of an object, such as his (or its height, requires only passive participation by the object of measure ment; we simply lay the ruler alongside the object being measured and read off the result. On the other hand, psychological properties, such as the amount of mechanical ability that a person has, or the amount of sensation generated by a pin prick administered with a certain amount of pressure, are *implicit* or *latent* properties. The evaluation of the amount of such psychological properties requires the active par ticipation of the subject; he must behave in the presence of one o more stimuli for us to be able to infer the amount of a psychological property, either possessed by the subject himself, or perceived by him as possessed by the stimulus. Presumably, the behaviors of one o more subjects faced with one or more stimuli contain a great deal o potential information about both the subjects and the stimuli. The way in which we gather and extract this information and, in particular the way in which behaviors are interpreted, dictates how values on the psychological property will be obtained. Psychological measuremen techniques, or scaling procedures, thus differ according to (1) the behav ioral task given to subjects, (2) the information implicit in the behavior that are actually called forth, and (3) the things that are assumed about the factors underlying the observed behaviors.

A great many measurement techniques exist in psychology, and it is both impossible and inappropriate to try to cover even a sizable number of such methods in an elementary presentation such as this On the other hand, it is informative to examine a few scaling or mea surement methods in some detail, with particular emphasis on the theoretical reasoning that underlies each method; in this way the heavy dependence of measurement procedures on both empirical evidence and theoretical assumptions becomes apparent. The techniques pre sented in the following sections were chosen to represent a fairly wide variety of problems, to be simple to understand, and to depend only upon a limited statistical and mathematical vocabulary. Much more advanced and systematic inventories of psychological measurement methods may be found in the volumes by Guilford (1954), Torgerson (1958), and Coombs (1964).

PSYCHOPHYSICS AND PSYCHOMETRICS

Conventionally, psychological measurement is discussed under two main headings: *psychophysics,* and *psychometrics.* Psychophysical methods were originally developed to study the relation between the physical properties of objects or stimuli and the sensation they produce— that is, the length, weight, numerosity, frequency, wavelength of objects, and the magnitude of *sensation* evoked by each. Historically psychophysics deals with the translation of physical characteristics of stimuli into their corresponding psychological characteristics. On the other hand, psychometrics traditionally deals with individual differences among people, in terms of purely psychological characteristics, such as intelligence, introversion-extroversion, degree of anxiety, and attitude-position. However, in modern psychological work, this distinction has almost broken down, since it is recognized that individual differences can be studied by traditional psychophysical methods and that certain methods growing out of the theory of mental tests apply quite well to problems of quite different stimulus and response relationships. Hence, only a very rough division of methods will be made here. The first concern will be with problems in which a number of different *stimuli* are to be scaled on a particular characteristic as judged from the responses of one or more subjects. Next, methods developed for the purpose of scaling a number of different *subjects* by their responses to a constant stimulus situation will be examined. Finally, a few methods will be considered in which *either or both* subject or stimuli are scaled. These methods will differ from each other primarily in the aspect of the situation that is varied or held constant and in the features of the situation that are scaled.

PSYCHOPHYSICAL METHODS

The psychological event corresponding to any given stimulus is not a simple mirror-like reflection of the event's physical properties. That this is true is borne out in a wide range of human behavior. For example, if an individual were asked to compare an object weighing 1 ounce with another weighing 5 ounces, he could almost certainly tell that the latter feels heavier than the former. On the other hand, if 4 ounces of flour were added to a sack that already weighed 200 pounds, one could rarely detect the difference in weight. And yet, physically, the difference in actual *weight* in these two situations is exactly the same. Furthermore, a blonde person is perceived as blonde whether he is standing in bright sunlight or in the murky light of a nightclub. The actual physical wavelengths of the light reflected by his hair may be very different under these two circumstances; but the average viewer would not ordinarily behave as though he noticed any difference. What then, are the connections between the physical properties of a stimulus and the psychological impact of the stimulus as determined by a subject's behavior? How can a physical scale of values be related to an accompanying psychological scale of values? This is the basic problem of psychophysics.

One of the very first of the quantitative measurement methods developed in psychology was the *method of just noticeable differences* which was originally designed to measure the amount of sensation experienced by a subject as a function of the physical intensity of the stimulus. This method, an example of a classical psychophysical method, rests both on a principle derived from empirical observation and on a theoretical assumption. The empirical principle was drawn from experiments first initiated by E. H. Weber (1795-1878). In his experiments, pairs of stimuli of varying differences in intensity of some physical property were presented to subjects. One member of each pair of stimuli was always constant; the other varied. For any given pair, Weber recorded the number of times a subject indicated that the comparison stimulus was more intense than the standard. Thus, he obtained the proportion of instances in which a given stimulus, S, was judged more intense than the constant stimulus, S_0. After many trials in which the same constant stimulus was used along with a range of other stimuli, the resulting responses by the subjects were displayed as a cumulative frequency curve, or ogive, as shown in Figure 1. Here, the horizontal axis represents the physical intensity of a stimulus S. The vertical axis is the proportion of trials for which S was judged as more intense than the standard. When the curve showed S to correspond to a proportion of .75, Weber defined the S value as *just noticeably different* from the standard S_0. The S value that is *just noticeably different* from S_0 is denoted by $S_0 + \triangle S$, where $\triangle S$ is the physical difference between S and S_0 when S is *just noticeably different*. After studying the responses of subjects to many different stimuli, Weber concluded that $\triangle S = KS_0$ over different values of S_0 (i.e., different intensities of the standard stimulus). The amount by which a stimulus must be different from the standard in order to be termed *just noticeably different* depends directly on the intensity of the standard. If the standard is not very intense, a small increment in stimulus intensity will tend to be noticed. If the standard is very intense, it will take an enormous increase in intensity for a change to be noticed. This finding became known as Weber's Law, and although it has many exceptions, it does apply relatively well to a fairly wide variety of stimuli. Notice that Weber's Law really relates two physical quantities: S_0 is the intensity of the standard stimulus in physical units and $\triangle S$ is an increment or increase in intensity in the same units necessary for the new stimulus intensity $S_0 + \triangle S$ to qualify as *just noticeably different*.

It remained for G. T. Fechner in the 1850s to extend Weber's finding into a method for actually scaling amounts of *sensation* produced by various stimuli of differing intensity. However, Fechner was able to do this only by use of a simple, but very important, theoretical assumption.

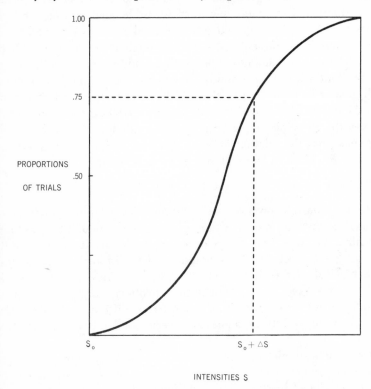

PROPORTIONS OF TRIALS

INTENSITIES S

$S_0 + \triangle S =$ INTENSITY JUST NOTICEABLY DIFFERENT FROM S

Figure 1

Ogive showing S just noticeably different from S_0.

Call R_0 the sensation evoked by S_0 and R_1 that evoked by S_1. Fechner assumed that *equally often noticed differences are psychologically equal*. This makes it possible to say that if stimulus S_1 is *just noticeably different* from S_0 and that if S_2 is *just noticeably different* from S_1, then sensation R_1 is just as different from R_0 as R_2 is from R_1. Fechner defined the *just noticeable difference* (or jnd) to be the unit of sensation, standing for least difference in sensation perceptible to a subject. Then, using the assumption that *equally often noticed differences are equal,* Fechner concluded that

$$\frac{\triangle S}{S_0} = \triangle R.$$

That is, the increase in sensation, or $\triangle R$, that accompanies an increase in intensity from S_0 to $S_0 + \triangle S$, is simply the ratio of $\triangle S$ to S_0. This means that if a stimulus of relatively low intensity is changed to a higher level (new level $= S_0 + \triangle S$), the change will produce a greater increase in sensation than if a stimulus of a higher original intensity had been changed by the same amount. For example, adding one candle power ($\triangle S$) of illumination to a stimulus (S_0) of five candle powers produces a much greater *increase* in sensation ($\triangle R$) than is produced by adding one candle power ($\triangle S$) to a stimulus already at 100 candle powers (S_0).

Given this principle, it was then possible to deduce the mathematical consequence that the relation between S values in units of stimulus intensity and R values in units of sensation must follow the rule:

$$R = C \log (S/L).$$

Here, C is a constant number and L is the *limen,* or the intensity of the stimulus at the lowest value capable of producing sensation. Graphically, this says that the relationship between stimulus intensity values and amounts of sensation should be of the form shown in Figure 2. Note that when this is true at the low intensities, a difference in intensity of any given size amounts to a relatively large difference in sensation. In the upper ranges of intensity, a difference of the same size between the stimuli amounts to a very small difference in sensation.

Again, for example, the difference in sensation produced by light sources at 10 and 20 candle powers should be much greater than the difference produced between 110 and 120 candle powers. For the subject, 10 and 20 candle powers should be seen as *more different* than 110 and 120 candle powers, even though the physical difference in terms of units of illumination is the same for both pairs of stimuli. Given the values of the necessary constants C and L, numerical values for the amount of sensation produced by these stimuli could actually be found.

Hence, Fechner showed one way of measuring a purely psychological characteristic that is associated with a stimulus—the amount of sensation it produces. This can be measured if the constant C is known along with the constant L (limen) for the particular subject and physical characteristic of the stimuli under study. Methods have been developed for the determination of the limen, L, and the necessary nstant, C; when these are available, sensation may be assigned a lue directly from the physical intensity value of the stimulus.

This is an excellent example of the dependence of a measurement chnique upon empirical evidence (which first suggested the princi- le embodied in Weber's Law) and on theoretical assumptions fol- wed by their mathematical consequences (as shown in Fechner's as- umption of the equality of *equally often noticed differences*).

Fechner's procedure was very important for the impetus it gave the search for quantitative methods in psychology. The work of echner explicitly demonstrated for the first time that a purely psycho- gical characteristic such as amount of sensation could be measured in derived way from the known physical intensity of the stimulus and

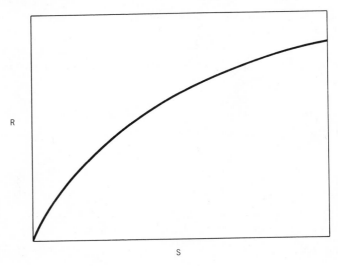

Figure 2

Graph of $R = C \log (S/L)$ for arbitrary values of C and L.

he behavior of the subject. Naturally, modern work in the area of sychophysics has gone very far beyond both the theory and the meth- ods developed by Fechner, and assumptions such as the *equality of equally often noticed differences* are now called seriously into question. Nevertheless, almost all of the quantitative methods in use today in psychology and in other social sciences point back, in one way or another, to the Fechnerian methods.

One very prominent modern alternative to the methods proposed by Fechner should be mentioned next. This is the method developed by S. S. Stevens (1957, 1958, 1959) for scaling stimuli with respect to a psychological characteristic. The method is introduced here as a par ticularly pertinent example of how a different experimental task, a dif ferent body of empirical evidence, and a different theoretical position can result in quite a different measurement technique.

Stevens takes the position that derived measurement in psychology can have the same character as derived measurement in the physical sciences in the sense that a characteristic such as temperature is reflected in quite a different continuum by means of a thermometer. The thermometer is a device for translating temperature into a scale of dis tance. In this same way, he argues, a subject can compare and contras stimuli that differ by a psychological quality, such as loudness, by mak ing comparable adjustments on some physical scale, such as length Indeed, Stevens produces evidence that subjects can express numerical values that correspond quite closely to magnitudes (or ratios of magni tudes) of intensity of stimuli. When subjects are given the task of judg ing the ratios of stimulus-intensity magnitudes as direct numerical ratios, Stevens finds that *equal physical ratios of stimulus intensity produce reports of equal ratios of subjective* (i.e., *sensation*) *magni tudes.*

Let us grant that when a subject reports such a numerical ratio, he reports a subjective or sensation ratio. This leads to the position that

$$\frac{\triangle S}{S_0} = \frac{\triangle R}{R_0}$$

The ratio of the increment in sensation $\triangle R$ relative to the initia sensation R_0 is the same as the ratio of the increment in stimulus intensity $\triangle S$ relative to the initial intensity S_0. This in turn leads to the following mathematical relationship between stimulus intensity (S) and magnitude of sensation (R):

$$C(S)^k = R$$

or that the magnitude of sensation is directly proportional to the mag nitude of the stimulus intensity raised to some constant power (k) the so-called *power law*. Graphically, this relation between S and F might appear as shown in Figure 2. Given experimental methods for determining the necessary constants C and R, the sensation value can be found directly from the stimulus intensity value, according to Stev ens' principles. Stevens' research suggests that the values of C and R vary according to the sense modality studied (vision, hearing, touch etc.) but that the general principle of the power law appears to fit a large range of such data.

Thus, the original Fechnerian theory (based on the idea of the equality of *equally often noticed differences*) and Stevens' theory (based on the equality of physical magnitude ratios and subjective magnitude ratios) yield different forms of relationship between stimulus and sensation. Which is correct? Either might be or neither might be, depending on the particular physical characteristic of the stimulus under study. Some of the extensive experimental evidence that considers this point will be covered in other volumes of this series. These two positions do not exhaust the theoretical possibilities for the relationship between stimulus intensity and magnitude of sensation or the tasks the subject might be given. Hence, there may well be other ways to measure sensation. However, for our immediate purposes, the Stevens and Fechner

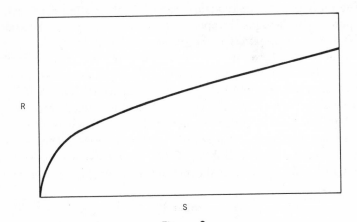

Figure 3

One possible power-law relationship between S and R of the form $R = CS^k$.

results provide good, relatively simple examples of the dependence of a procedure for the measurment of a psychological property on both empirical and theoretical considerations.

PSYCHOLOGICAL SCALING WITHOUT A PHYSICAL PROPERTY

The traditional psychophysical problem is the relationship of a psychological event, such as sensation, to some known physical characteristic of the stimulus, such as its intensity. However, very often one wishes to measure some psychological charactertistic of stimuli when no explicit physical features can be singled out. For example, one might wish to measure the worth a subject puts on each of a variety of objects. The worth of any object may depend on a great number of physical characteristics. Or, perhaps, one might wish to measure the perceived similarity of *pairs* of objects. Similarity may be perceived by the sub-

ject on any number of physical dimensions. Or, perhaps we wish to measure the perceived *smoothness* of each of a set of objects. Smoothness
describes a psychological, not a simple physical continuum. The methods
to be discussed next still apply if there is some obvious physical characteristic that distinguishes the objects of judgment. Nevertheless, for
these methods the presence or absence of such a physical property is
irrelevant.

PAIR COMPARISONS AND THE LAW OF COMPARATIVE JUDGMENT

The most popular method for scaling a set of stimuli according to
some purely psychological property is the *method of pair comparisons*
and the *Law of Comparative Judgment* developed by L. L. Thurstone
(1927). Suppose there are an N number of separate and distinct
objects to be scaled on some property—say, their perceived heaviness.
These objects are presented to the subject in all of the $(N)(N-1)/2$
paired combinations. For each combination, the subject reports which
member of the pair he judges to be the heavier. Each possible pair is
presented not just once but a sizable number of times. The results can
then be put into a form resembling Table 1, which shows the proportion
of times the object shown in the column was judged heavier than the
object shown in the row. For example, in this table it is shown that object

Table 1

*Proportions of times that the column stimulus was
judged heavier than the row stimulus.*

	A	B	C	D	E
A	.50	.81	.23	.47	.61
B	.19	.50	.06	.17	.28
C	.77	.94	.50	.74	.85
D	.53	.83	.26	.50	.64
E	.39	.72	.15	.36	.50

object shown in the row. For example, in this table it is shown that object
B was judged heavier than object A .81 proportion of the time. The
numbers .50 are inserted arbitrarily in the matching diagonal cells of the
table, since ordinarily an object is not compared with itself.

Now in order to obtain scale values for the stimulus objects from
such data, Thurstone assumed that each object does in fact have some
true scale position in terms of the psychological characteristic under
study. Thus, any object i will have some true value, x_i. However, he also
assumed that at the moment of judgment t there may have been a certain
amount of error, or deviation (e_{it}) from the true position and that the

ubject behaved as though the value of object i were $x_i + e_{it}$ rather than x_i. Furthermore, he assumed that the error values for any given stimulus were normally distributed with a mean of zero and a variance of σ_i^2. Thus, the distribution of values $x_i + e_{it}$ over all possible judging occasions appears as in Figure 4. Thurstone called this concept of a distribution of values about some central, true, value of the stimulus a *discriminal dispersion*. He based the assumption that the distribution of errors should be *normal* on the well-known principle that errors due to the combination of large numbers of purely chance factors do tend to be distributed in this way.

Let the difference between the perceived positions of two stimuli, i and j, be defined as follows for any given time t:

$$d_{ij} = (x_i + e_{it}) - (x_j + e_{jt}).$$

The true (average) difference between i and j is simply $x_i - x_j$. Now it will be useful to recall the following principles you have already encountered in statistics:

1. If a variable, e_{it}, is normally distributed with variance σ^2 and mean of zero, then if x_i is a constant, the variable $x_i + e_{it}$ will be normally distributed with variance σ^2 and mean x_i.

2. If e_{it} and e_{jt} are both normally distributed, each with mean zero and variances σ_i^2 *and* σ_j^2, respectively, then their difference, $e_{it} - e_{jt}$ will be normally distributed with mean of zero and with variance:

$$\sigma_i^2 + \sigma_j^2 - 2 \text{ Cov } (e_{it}, e_{jt}).$$

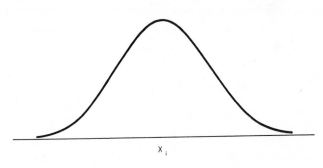

$$X_i$$

Figure 4

Normal-curve distribution of values of $x_i + e_{it}$ *with mean at* x_j.

Here, Cov (e_{it}, e_{jt}) stands for the covariance of e_{it} and e_{jt}, or $r_{ij}\,\sigma_i\,\sigma_j$; it thus reflects the interdependence or correlation between e_{it} and e_{jt} over times (t).

Now at any moment t in time, the difference between the perceived magnitude of stimulus i and of stimulus j should be

$$d_{ij} = (x_i + e_{it}) - (x_j + e_{jt}) = (x_i - x_j) + (e_{it} - e_{jt}),$$

and by our previous assumptions the distribution of such differences should be normal. Furthermore, the mean difference between two such variables is given by the difference between their means so that on the average the difference in perceived magnitude between stimuli i and j is just $x_i - x_j$. In statistics it is shown that the variance of the difference between two random variables is the *sum* of their respective variances minus twice their covariance. Also, the distribution of perceived differences d_{ij} between stimulus i and stimulus j must have a variance given by

$$\text{Var } (d_{ij}) = \sigma_i^2 + \sigma_j^2 - 2 \text{ Cov } (e_{it}, e_{jt}).$$

Finally, given that all of the above is true, the proportion of times that stimulus i is judged greater than stimulus j must correspond to the area cut off under a normal curve by the value

$$d_{ij} = (x_i - x_j) + (e_{it} - e_{jt}). = 0,$$

since i will be judged greater than j only when the difference $(x_i - x_j) + (e_{it} - e_{jt})$, is greater than or equal to zero. This means that the standardized value (z_{ij}), corresponding to the proportion cut off under a normal curve equal to the proportion of times that i was judged greater than j, must itself equal

$$z_{ij} = (0 - x_i + x_j) \left/ \sqrt{\sigma_i^2 + \sigma_j^2 - 2 \text{ Cov } (e_{it}, e_{jt})} \right.$$

or

$$x_j - x_i = z_{ij} \left/ \sqrt{\sigma_i^2 + \sigma_i^2 \, 2 \text{ Cov } (e_{it}, e_{jt})}. \right.$$

Hence, since z_{ij} can be found directly from the obtained proportion of judgments, if enough is known or can be assumed about the values of the variances and the covariance, the true difference between x_j and x_i can be obtained.

Of course, values such as σ_i^2 and σ_j^2 are not ordinarily known. The simplest solution to this problem of the unknown variances and covariances is called Thurstone's Case V solution. Here, one simply assumes that the term

$$\sigma_i^2 + \sigma_j^2 - 2 \text{ Cov } (e_{it}, e_{jt})$$

is constant and equal to unity over all possible i *and* j *pairs of stimuli.* Given this assumption, the required scale values can be found directly by a simple process of averaging the z values obtained from the proportions of judgments (i.e., scale value = mean z value).

For example, normal-curve tables provide the information in Table 2 which shows the z (or standardized) value required to cut off the area corresponding to any given proportion in Table 1 above. Thus, the value .87 in the row A and the column B of this table indicates that a z value of approximately .87 is required to cut off the *lower* .81 proportion of area in a normal curve, where the proportion .81 was found from the corresponding cell in Table 1. Similarly, the value .28 was found from the normal table to correspond to the proportion .61 as shown in the cell for column E and row A in Table 1. In short, Table 2 shows the approximate normal z equivalents of the proportions

Table 2

Standardized normal values corresponding to the proportions in Table 1.

	A	B	C	D	E	
A	0	.87	−.73	−.08	.28	
B	−.87	0	−1.60	−.96	−.58	
C	.73	1.60	0	.65	1.02	
D	.08	.96	−.65	0	.37	
E	−.28	.58	−.102	−.37	0	
	−.34	4.01	−4.00	−.76	1.09	Σz
	−.068	.802	−.800	−.152	.218	$M_z = $ scale value

given in Table 1, as referred to a normal curve. Then, the scale value for each stimulus is found simply by taking the average z value in its column as shown at the bottom of Table 2. If all of the assumptions are true, this produces a scale of the stimulus magnitude in terms of the psychological characteristic under consideration. The five stimuli, together with their values in terms of psychological heaviness, are graphed in Figure 5. The mean value for the objects receives the value

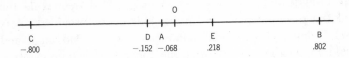

Figure 5

Scale values of stimuli found from Table 2.

zero, and the unit of measurement can be interpreted to be *one standard deviation of perceived difference between stimuli.*

The Thurstone method of stimulus scaling by the method of pair comparisons and by his Law of Comparative Judgment has been very widely applied in psychological research. Almost any objects of judgment can be scaled on virtually any psychological characteristic by this method. Nevertheless, there is one very important proviso: Pairs of the objects must not be so different from each other or so completely discriminable from each other as to give proportions that are very nearly 0 or very nearly 1.00. Scale values for such completely discriminable objects or stimuli cannot be found directly by this particular method. Modifications of Thurstone's method do exist for this situation, however, and the reader is referred to Guilford (1954) or to Torgerson (1958) for their discussion. Furthermore, the application of the method of pair comparisons becomes experimentally cumbersome when there are very many stimuli to be judged, since the number of possible pairs and hence the number of necessary judgments by the subject, becomes extremely large. In addition, since judgments for any given pair must be repeated many times, practice and fatigue effects on the subjects can have a considerable influence on the scale values obtained. Although this method is frequently used for a situation where each subject judges each pair only once and where the data for many subjects are pooled, this does require additional assumptions about the distributions and variances of perceived values across subjects. Yet, in spite of these drawbacks, Thurstone's methods, such as this and its near relatives, have been extremely influential in the development of psychological measurement.

At this point, it is well to emphasize that although the stimuli so far referred to have been physical objects such as weights, there is absolutely nothing in the formal construction of the Thurstone scaling procedure that keeps it from being applied even when persons are themselves the stimuli for judgment by other persons. Thus, one might wish to scale a group of people on the attribute of good sportsmanship. In this case, one could present the stimulus people in pairs to a single judge or a group of judges and then scale them in terms of the resulting pair-comparison judgments, provided, of course, that each judge had some reasonable basis for his judgment and that one could reasonably assume that the theoretical requirements of the method were met. Formally, the methods do not depend either on the nature of the stimuli or on the nature of the characteristics on which they are compared. However, if uninformed judges are asked to make comparisons on nonsense characteristics, one can hardly expect the results to be meaningful.

A METHOD BASED ON RANK ORDERS

A very frequently applied method of securing judgments of a set of objects or people is to ask one or more judges to *rank order* the stimuli according to some particular characteristics. For example, ten objects of art might be ranked by one or more judges according to beauty, which is certainly a psychological rather than a purely physical characteristic. Suppose that only a single judge is employed and that he assigns ranks as follows:

RANK	OBJECT
1	C
2	E
3	A
4	D
5	F
6	H
7	G
8	J
9	I
10	B

The ranks given to the several objects may be interpreted as showing that the true magnitude of beauty that the judge perceives for object C is greater than the magnitude he perceives for object E. This is in turn greater than the magnitude he perceives for object A. However, without further assumptions about how the judge goes about assigning ranks to perceived magnitudes of objects, one cannot say that the *difference* in beauty between object C and object E is exactly the same as the *difference* between E and A, merely because the ordinal positions of C and E and of E and A each appear to be one place apart. On the other hand, if one can make a reasonable assumption about the relation of ranks to values, it may be possible to convert such ranks into interval-scale values representing amounts of beauty for each object as perceived by the judge.

One common assumption made in order to convert ranks to such numerical scores is that *true differences between adjacent objects ranked near the extremes tend to be larger than differences between objects falling near the middle in rank.* In particular, we might think of the relative differences among the objects ranked as being similar to differences between the standardized or z values falling at the boundary points of $N-1$ equally probable intervals falling in the midrange of a normal distribution. Such intervals are exemplified in Figure 6. We would like the interval between the stimulus ranked 1 and the stimulus ranked 2 to cut exactly $100/N$ percent of the cases in a normal distribution. Similarly, we would like the interval between the stimulus ranked 2 and the one ranked 3 to define an interval corresponding to $100/N$ of cases in a normal distribution. The interval between other adjacent ranks should cut off $100/N$ percent of cases in a normal distribution as well. Finally, we arbitrarily set $100/2N$ as the proportion of cases in a normal distribution to be cut below the value of the stimulus ranked 1 and $100/2N$ as the percent of cases above the value of the stimulus ranked N. This assumption will make the score difference between the objects ranked 1 and 2 greater than the difference between the objects ranked 2 and 3 which will in turn be greater than the difference between the objects ranked

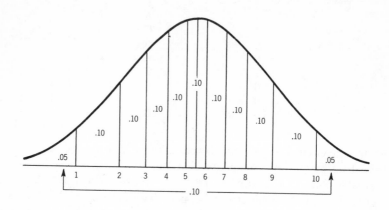

Figure 6

Division of normal curve into equally probable intervals corresponding to differences in ranks.

3 and 4. On the other hand, for ten stimulus objects the difference between the objects ranked 10 and 9 will be greater than the difference between the objects ranked 9 and 8, and so on.

On making this admittedly arbitrary assumption, we can proceed as follows: For any object falling at rank j, we find from the normal tables the z score cutting off the lower $(j-.5)/N$ proportion of the area under the normal curve. Thus, for object C, we find that the lower $(1-.5)/10$ or .05 proportion of the area under the normal curve corresponds to a z value of -1.65. Hence, this value is assigned to object C. Next, for object E, the $(2-.5)/10$ or .15 proportion corresponds to a z of -1.04. This, then, is the value assigned to object E. Proceeding in this way, we find the following z values corresponding to the objects:

OBJECT	RANK	PERCENTILE	z VALUE
C	1	5	−1.65
E	2	15	−1.04
A	5	25	− .67
D	4	35	− .39
F	5	45	− .13
H	6	55	.13
G	7	65	.39
J	8	75	.67
I	9	85	1.04
B	10	95	1.65

Here, then, we have translated the original ranks into values, having the property of relatively large differences among objects ranked at the extremes and small differences among objects ranked in the middle groups. Naturally, if the rank 1 originally indicated "most beautiful," we would want to reverse the signs of these values. On the other hand, if 1 represented "least beautiful," the signs might reasonably be allowed to stand as they are.

This procedure is really quite arbitrary and rests only on the presupposition that extreme differences in value for adjacent objects should be likely to occur when those objects are ranked at the extreme and that relatively small differences should occur when the objects are in a medial position to the rest. Fortunately, we very seldom ask only one

Table 3

Rankings given to ten objects by fifty judges.

OBJECT	A	B	C	D	E	F	G	H	I	J	z
RANK											
1	20	6	2	12	0	0	0	10	0	0	−1.65
2	6	5	27	10	2	0	0	0	0	0	−1.04
3	2	27	15	6	0	0	0	0	0	0	− .67
4	12	10	6	7	15	0	0	0	0	0	− .39
5	10	0	0	15	17	8	0	0	0	0	− .13
6	0	0	0	0	10	17	21	2	0	0	.13
7	0	0	0	0	0	10	7	33	0	0	.39
8	0	0	0	0	6	0	10	5	27	2	.67
9	0	0	0	0	0	15	12	0	23	0	1.04
10	0	2	0	0	0	0	0	0	0	48	1.65

	−.931		−.875		−.096		.493		.840	
		−.676		−.778		.413		−.0004		1.61

scale = average z
value   value

judge for his rank order, and when a fairly large number of judges provide a ranking of the same objects, this procedure becomes somewhat more reasonable.

Suppose, now, that 50 judges had provided rank orders of the same ten objects. Then results could be put into a table similar to Table 3. Here, a column of the table symbolizes a particular object. The entry in a cell of the table shows how many subjects gave the object shown by the column the rank shown by the row. In this table, the entry of 20 in row 1 and the column marked A indicates that 20 subjects assigned rank 1 to the object A. The entry of 15 in the row 5 and the column for object D shows that 15 subjects assigned rank 5 to object D, and so on for the other cells.

Once again we assume that the difference in extreme ranks for an individual subject tends to reflect a larger perceived difference between objects than does an equivalent difference among the middle ranks. Then, the boundary z values of intervals cutting off equal areas under the normal curve are substituted for the ranks themselves exactly as before. These z values are shown in the last column of Table 3. Finally, the scale value for each object is found simply by taking its average z value. Thus,

$$X_A = \frac{-1.65(20) -1.04(6) -.67(2) -.39(12) -.13(10)}{50} = -.931;$$

$$X_B = \frac{-1.65(6) -1.04(5) -.67(27) -.39(10) +1.65(2)}{50} = -.676.$$

The scale values for the other objects are found in a similar way. The net result is that objects the judges agree are extreme in rank receive extreme scale values. (An example is object J.) On the other hand, objects consistently ranked in the midpositions or about which there is great disagreement among the judges receive score values near zero. (Compare objects E and H, for example.)

There are other considerably more refined methods for scaling objects from rank orders given by judges. Perhaps the most satisfactory and justifiable method is to convert ranks into a form equivalent to pair comparisons and then to apply the Thurstone Law of Comparative Judgment procedures. However, the method of converting ranks to z scores and averaging, as just shown, is computationally much simpler and gives results in quite good agreement with the pair-comparison methods. Hence, since rank orders are generally easier to secure from judges than are all possible pair comparisons, and since results of this method just shown are approximately like those arrived at by converting ranks to equivalent pair comparisons, this method of converting ranks to score values is probably worthy of use for many purposes. Like the results of Thurstone scaling, the objects judged can be thought of as measured on an interval scale where the unit is *one standard deviation* in the distribution of true values over all possible objects on this scale. The zero point on this scale corresponds to the mean value over all objects.

A METHOD OF SUCCESSIVE INTERVALS

Still another method based on the normal distribution is often quite useful when a large number of objects are judged either by a single subject or by a group of subjects. In such situations the number of possible pair comparisons among stimulus objects is usually prohibitively large. Furthermore, subjects ordinarily find it extremely difficult to rank order large numbers of objects. Thus, in such situations another procedure for collecting and analyzing data is called for.

Consider the situation in which one subject has the task of judging a relatively large number of objects on some psychological dimension. He may, for example, be judging a set of 200 attitude statements on the basis of their liberal versus their conservative tone. Or he may be judging a set of his peers on the basis of outgoing personality versus withdrawn personality. Or he may be faced with any of a large variety of similar judgment tasks. Rather than compare the stimulus objects by pairs or by rank order, this time the judge has the task of placing each object in the appropriate *category* or *interval*. That is, in the attitude judgment situation the subject may be required to judge the attitude items according to some convenient number of categories such as very liberal, moderately liberal, intermediate, moderately conservative, or very conservative. In another instance he may be required to judge the degree of outgoing personality shown by his peers according to such categories as thoroughly outgoing, mostly outgoing, more outgoing than withdrawn, equally outgoing and withdrawn, more withdrawn than outgoing, mostly withdrawn, or thoroughly withdrawn. The point is that some relatively small number of categories is provided (generally an odd number) and that these categories are successive in the sense that they form some logical progression by *degree* of the characteristic under study.

Suppose, for example, that the subject is given 50 objects to classify according to seven categories on the basis of beauty. He is to denote the categories simply by the numbers 1 through 7. The number 1 is to mean not beautiful at all, and 7 is to mean very beautiful. The objects are then given to the subject in some random order, and his job is to classify each object according to the category he judges most appropriate. The results might appear as shown in Table 4.

Table 4

Categories, proportions, and scale values.

Category	1	2	3	4	5	6	7
p	.02	.08	.30	.12	.37	.07	.04
cp	.02	.10	.40	.52	.89	.96	1.00
Boundary value	-2.05 X_{12}	-1.28 X_{23}	$-.25$ X_{34}	$.05$ X_{45}	1.23 X_{56}	1.75 X_{67}	
Mean value of interval	-2.440	-1.587	$-.703$	$-.097$	$.572$	1.438	2.157

The first row in this table gives the category number; the second, the *proportion* of the total set of objects assigned to each category; and the third row, the *cumulative proportion* for that category (i.e., the proportionate number assigned in that category *or below*).

As always, in order to go from such data to scale values for the objects, one must make some theoretical assumptions. In this instance we will assume that the *true* values for the stimulus objects are approximately normally distributed. This assumption makes it possible first to scale the *category boundaries* between the successive categories and then to arrive at corresponding stimulus values. Consider first the boundary between the intervals or categories 1 and 2. This boundary has a value X_{12} that must be greater than or equal to the value for any stimulus object placed in category 1 but less than that for any object placed in category 2. We know from Table 4 that only 2 percent of the objects fall below X_{12} in true value. Hence, since one assumes a normal distribution of values, the normal table tells us that in standard or z-score form $X_{12} = -2.05$. Any object placed in category 1 is assigned a value less than or equal to -2.05, which is the upper boundary for that category. Next, we consider the boundary X_{23} between category 2 and category 3. At or below this point fall 10 percent of objects. Hence, the normal table shows that X_{23} must correspond to a z score of -1.28. Any objects placed in category 2 will then have a value in z-score form that is greater than -2.05 but less than or equal to -1.28. Proceeding in this way, we find all of the category boundary values. These are shown as the fourth row in Table 4. The boundaries of each category correspond to z scores that bound particular areas in a normal distribution. Note that this makes the *width* of each category depend both on the proportion of cases it includes *and* its position among all of the categories.

However, what value shall we assign to the actual objects that were placed into each of the categories? It seems reasonable to give an object the mean value of the category into which it is placed. The procedure for finding these mean values for intervals is given by another property of the normal distribution. In a normal distribution, the *mean value* for any given interval of z values can be found from the following expression:

$$\text{mean of interval} = \frac{(\text{density at lower limit}) - (\text{density at upper limit})}{(\text{area below upper limit}) - (\text{area below lower limit})}.$$

Application of this principle thus yields the mean value for any category or interval in which cases fall. (Recall that normal tables ordinarily give both areas or proportions cut off by various z values as well as the height of the normal curve, or density, at each such value.) For example, category 1 has a lower limit only at an infinite negative value, since it is an extreme, and hence open, interval. The density at the lower limit of any such open interval can then be taken as zero. Also, the area beneath the normal curve at or beyond this infinite point would be zero. However, the normal table shows that at a z score of -2.05 (the value of the upper limit, or x_{12}) the density is approximately .0488 in a normal distribution. Table 4 shows that at or below x_{12} lie only .02 of the total number of cases. Hence, *the mean value in category* 1 is found to be:

$$\frac{0 - .0488}{.02 - 0} = -2.440.$$

Consequently, any object placed into category 1 will be assigned this mean value, or -2.44.

Next, one must consider the objects in category 2. First, one finds that the density value associated with X_{23}, or -1.28, is approximately .1758 and that the proportion placed at or below X_{23} is .10. Furthermore, the density at the lower limit, or X_{12}, is .0488. Thus, the mean value for objects falling into category 2 should be:

$$\frac{.0488 - .1758}{.10 - .02} = -1.587.$$

The value -1.587 is the mean z value for objects in category 2, and this value is assigned to all objects placed in that category. One proceeds in this way up to category 7. Here, the upper limit to this open interval must be infinite and would have a density of zero. Furthermore, the upper limit to this interval would bound 100 percent of the area of a normal curve. The mean value for this interval would be:

$$\frac{.0863 - 0}{1.00 - .96} = 2.157.$$

Each object placed in category 7 is thus given the mean value for that category, or 2.157. The resultant mean value for each of the categories is shown in Table 4. If an object is judged to fall into a particular category, the object is given the category value.

Although on occasion it may be useful to employ this method of successive intervals on data from only a single subject, it is well to remember that the scale values found in this manner refer to the psychological characteristic of the objects *according to that subject*. There are no grounds at all for assuming that another subject would show the same, or even a similar, distribution of the objects over the categories. If the point at issue were the similarity among subjects in their views of these objects, it might then be useful to scale the objects by successive intervals for each subject and then to compare and correlate subjects over stimulus values. Furthermore, if each subject had independently assigned the objects to categories and the scaling had been carried out by this method separately for each subject, it is possible to assign a composite scale value for each object by taking the mean value over subjects. However, for even a moderately large number of subjects, this can amount to a great deal of computation. This method is probably best reserved for situations in which each of a small group of subjects judges a fairly large number of objects and the stimulus scale values are estimated separately for each subject. Nevertheless, this method can also be useful in situations in which a large number of subjects judge only one object by categorizing it among successive intervals. This situation will be discussed further under *rating scale methods*.

THE LAW OF CATEGORICAL JUDGMENT

The most usual situation in psychology calls for some relatively large number of subjects each to categorize some fairly large number of stimuli. The end product desired is a scale value for each stimulus. These values represent a consensual position for each stimulus according to the particular group of subjects employed. This situation, in which many stimuli are assigned to successive intervals by many judges, is best handled by a somewhat different set of assumptions and a different method of analysis than the ones discussed above. Suppose, for example, that 100 subjects classify six stimuli among the same seven categories used in the previous example according to the characteristic of beauty. In this instance the data could be put into the form shown in Table 5 as follows:

Table 5

Category boundary

OBJECT	(1,2)	(2,3)	(3.4)	(4,5)	(5,6)	(6,7)
A	.02	.10	.35	.50	.86	.94
B	.10	.22	.43	.62	.76	.89
C	.01	.18	.50	.64	.73	.90
D	.05	.46	.48	.64	.78	.90
E	.01	.02	.10	.25	.62	.85
F	.03	.05	.05	.56	.94	.98

In this table the stimulus objects are shown as the rows, and the category boundaries are shown as columns. Any cell of the table shows the proportion of subjects who classified the object *at or below* the given category boundary. Thus, for example, object A was placed in category 1 by only 2 percent of the subjects. This means 2 percent of the subjects placed the value of A at or below the boundary between categories 1 and 2, or x_{12}. Similarly, 10 percent of the subjects placed object A either in category 1 or 2, implying that 10 percent judged the value of A to be below the boundary between category 2 and category 3 or x_{23}.

In treating such data, one might assume that the value x_{iA} assigned by subject i to any stimulus A is normally distributed across subjects. That is, the various psychological values perceived by different subjects for any given stimulus is assumed to be distributed normally. The true value of stimulus A, or X_A, is the *mean* of this normal distribution. Similar distributions and means are assumed for each of the other objects. Furthermore, one also assumes that the perceived location of the boundary between any two adjacent categories, such as x_{i12} for categories 1 and 2 is normally distributed over subject i. From these assumptions, it follows that the proportion of times that stimulus A was placed in category 1 corresponds to an area under a normal curve with mean $(X_A - x_{12})$ and with a variance of σ^2, depending both on the variance of the x_{Ai} values and the variance of the x_{i12} values. A further assumption that the variance of each boundary distribution is the same, together with the assumption that the degree of dependency of the stimulus position on the boundary position is constant, makes the scaling procedure quite simple. We will find both the true boundary positions, such as x_{12}, and the true stimulus positions, such as X_A. (Obviously, these assumptions represent an extension of Thurstone's Law of Comparative Judgment, to the categorical-judgment situation. These theoretical assumptions are sometimes called the Law of Categorical Judgment.)

Granted that these normal-distribution assumptions are true, we can proceed as follows: First, one determines the z, or normal standardized, value that corresponds to each of the proportions in Table 5. These values are shown in Table 6. For example, the z value -2.05 for stimulus A and the category boundary $(1, 2)$ corresponds to the proportion .02 in Table 4, since approximately .02 of the area of a normal curve lies below $z = -2.05$. The other z values also correspond to the respective proportions in Table 5. Next, one finds the values of the category boundaries by taking the average value of each column in Table 6. That is, category-boundary value = mean z value over a column. Thus, for boundary $(1,2)$ the value is found from the following:

$$\frac{(-2.05) + (-1.28) + (-2.33) + (-1.65) + (-2.33) + (-1.88)}{6} = -1.92.$$

Table 6

Category boundary

OBJECT	(1,2)	(2,3)	(3,4)	(4,5)	(5,6)	(6,7)	SCALE VALUE
A	−2.05	−1.28	− .39	.00	1.08	1.55	−.043
B	−1.28	− .77	− .18	.31	.71	1.23	−.228
C	−2.33	− .92	.00	.36	.61	1.28	−.058
D	−1.65	− .10	− .05	.13	.77	1.28	−.288
E	−2.33	−2.05	−1.28	−.67	.31	1.04	.605
F	−1.88	−1.65	−1.65	.15	1.56	2.05	.012
Boundary value	−1.92	−1.13	− .59	.05	.84	1.40	

Mean boundary value $= -.225$

Values for the different category boundaries appear along the bottom margin of Table 6. These obtained values are actually the true category-boundary values minus the mean of all of the stimulus values. However, we will arbitrarily set the mean of the stimulus values equal to 0. This makes the column averages in Table 6 directly represent the category-boundary values. Next, we find the *average category boundary* by summing the values just found across all category boundaries and by dividing by the number of boundaries:

$$\text{average category boundary} = \frac{-1.92 - 1.13 - .59 + .05 + .84 + 1.40}{6} = -.225.$$

To determine the value associated with each stimulus one must average the z values in any given row of Table 6. This represents:

average of row A = (average category boundary) − (value for A).

Therefore, the value for stimulus A is found by taking the average of row A, changing the sign, and adding the average category boundary value:

$$\text{value for A} = \frac{-(-2.05 - 1.28 - .39 + 1.08 + 1.55)}{6} + (-.225) = -.043.$$

In the same way, one finds that the value for B is determined as follows:

$$\text{value for B} = \frac{-(-1.28 - .77 - .18 + .31 + .71 + 1.23)}{6} + (-.225) = -.228.$$

The calculation is repeated for the remaining stimulus objects. The values found by following this procedure for all the different stimulus objects are shown as the last column in Table 6. Note that the average stimulus value is 0.00. Apart from rounding error, this will always be true. These stimulus values can be viewed as on an interval scale with the 0 point corresponding to the average stimulus value and the unit of measurement equal to:

$$\sigma = \sqrt{\sigma^2_{\text{stimulus}} + \sigma^2_{\text{boundary}} - \text{Cov (stim, bound)}}$$

(This is the standard deviation of the difference between a stimulus and a boundary, which we have assumed constant over stimuli and boundaries, and a set equal to unity.) If we desire a more convenient set of numerical values for the stimuli, we can quite arbitrarily transform the original values by multiplying by any convenient positive constant and adding any chosen constant.

The procedure shown here for successive interval judgments pooled across judges is only the simplest of a variety of procedures that might be used on such data. The reader is referred to Torgerson (1958) for a complete exposition of such methods.

In summary, data based on the assignment of objects to successive categories or intervals may be turned into scale values for stimuli rather easily, either by the assumption of a normal distribution of true values or by the assumption of normal distributions both for the perceived values of a stimulus and for any category boundary over judges. Such data are easy to collect. These methods make stimulus scaling on almost any meaningful psychological characteristic fairly simple. However, like the pair-comparison method of Thurstone, which these methods strongly resemble, the results are only as good as the statistical assumptions on which they are based. Some empirical evidence does exist on the validity of the normal assumption when applied to judgment of objects; but, of course, there is no guarantee that such assumption will necessarily be appropriate in all contexts or situations. Blind or haphazard application of a scaling technique to data can never substitute for a careful study of the validity of the assumptions on which the technique is based. On the other hand, methods based on the normal assumption do seem to be both justified and practically useful in a fairly wide range of application.

THE SCALING OF PERSONAL VALUE, OR UTILITY

Before we leave the topic of stimulus scaling, one more potential method should be mentioned, not so much because it provides a currently popular or useful method but because it is based on quite a different set of behaviors on the part of the subject and because the theoretical justification for the method is rather different from those just discussed. This is a method for scaling the *utility* of three or more objects. Utility means the amount of personal value or goodness associated with objects. For example, a hungry person might have the choice of three different things to eat. Presumably each item has some value or utility for him as foodstuffs. Obviously, he would prefer a large delectable steak to a bowl of thin soup. And he would prefer the soup to a hard crust of stale bread. The person acts as though each of these objects has some utility value for him in the light of his needs. We might like to go further and try to determine how much more valuable the steak is to a person than the soup.

In another situation a tired businessman may have the choice of going to a literary tea, attending a musical comedy, or going directly to bed. Each of these acts should also have some utility value for the person. How much more utility to the person has the musical comedy over the literary tea? In still another situation a bidder at an auction may not hesitate to go from a bid of $100 to a bid of $101, but he may be reluctant to raise a bid of $1 to a bid of $2. He acts as though the value, or utility, to him of the additional $1 were different when added to $100 as opposed to $1. What is the utility value of an amount of money as distinct from its numerical dollar value?

Suppose there were three objects, A, B, and C, and that we wished to assign utility values to these objects according to a subject's preference behavior toward them. First of all, we can find out which object is most preferred by the subject, which is next most preferred, and finally which is least preferred. Presumably, the most preferred object has highest utility, the second most preferred has next highest utility, and the least preferred the lowest utility. Suppose that A is most preferred, B is next most preferred, and C least preferred.

Not only can we offer to give any object to the subject, we can also give him the option of so-called lotteries for pairs of the objects.

For example, the subject may be allowed to play a game, or participate in a lottery, in which he will receive the object A as a prize with probability 1/2 and the object B as prize with probability 1/2. That is, we might toss a coin to see if he gets object A or object B. Or, perhaps, we might give him the option of getting object B with probability 1/10 and object C with probability 9/10. Not only can we discuss the objects themselves but also all possible lotteries or gambling situations in which two or more of the objects appear as prizes with particular known probabilities. The person may express preferences not only between the objects themselves (lotteries with the particular object as a sure-thing prize) but also between different lotteries. This implies that the lotteries themselves must also have utility values for him. We assume that the value of a lottery with prizes such as A and C, with probabilities such as p and $1 - p$, is given by the *expected utility*, or the *expected value*, of that lottery. This expected utility is simply the utility of each possibility that might occur multiplied by the probability that it will occur and summed over all the possibilities. Thus, if the subject can get A with probability p or can get C with probability $1 - p$,

$$\text{utility of lottery} = (\text{utility of A})p + (\text{utility of C}) (1 - p).$$

The same procedure is followed for other objects and other probabilities.

Suppose that we have the objects A, B, and C, in that order of preference, and we ask the subject, "Would you rather have B for sure, or play a lottery in which you get A with probability 1/2 and C with probability 1/2?" If the subject prefers B over the lottery, then we know that:

$$\text{utility of B} > (\text{utility of A}) (1/2) + (\text{utility of C}) (1/2).$$

Otherwise, if he prefers to play the lottery:

$$\text{utility of B} < (\text{utility of A}) (1/2) + (\text{utility of C}) (1/2).$$

One could offer him the same option with any other lottery, say A with probability 2/3 and C with probability 1/3. If he still prefers B over the lottery, then:

$$\text{utility of B} > (\text{utility of A}) (2/3) + (\text{utility of C}) (1/3).$$

The same procedure is followed for any such lottery. Suppose that one kept adjusting the values of p and $1 - p$ until a lottery was found in which the subject is *indifferent* to B. That is, the subject is completely indifferent to the option of getting B for sure or playing this particular lottery. He has no preference between B and this lottery. This means that:

$$\text{(utility of B)} = \text{(utility of A)}p + \text{(utility of C)}\,(1-p).$$

Once this lottery indifferent to B has been found (i.e., the probabilities p and $1-p$ have been found, making him indifferent between B and the lottery for A and C) then the utility of B relative to A and C may also be found. Let A, the most preferred object, equal 1, and let C, the least preferred, equal 0. Then it follows that:

$$\text{(utility of B)} = (1)p + (0)\,(1-p) = p.$$

The difference in utility between B and C is in the proportion p to the difference between A and C. For example, if the subject is indifferent to B for sure as against the lottery that gives object A with probability 3/4 and C with probability 1/4, then:

$$\text{utility of B} = 3/4.$$

Here the utility difference between B and C is 3/4 of the difference between A and C. If A and C differ by 1, B and C differ by 3/4.

In principle, given three or more objects, one can find the utility values of all of these objects, relative to the most and least preferred, by exploring the values of p and $1-p$ leading to no preference, or indifference, between any object and a lottery. If, for example, utility values of five objects were known to be as follows, then lotteries for A and E must exist, and they should produce indifference as compared to each object. These would involve the following probabilities:

Table 7

OBJECT	TRUE UTILITY	INDIFFERENT LOTTERY IN TERMS OF A AND E
A	7.0	$p = 1.00, 1 - p = \ \ .00$
B	5.0	$p = \ \ .69, 1 - p = \ \ .31$
C	4.0	$p = \ \ .53, 1 - p = \ \ .47$
D	1.5	$p = .154, 1 - p = \ \ .846$
E	.5	$p = \ \ .00, 1 - p = 1.00$

The subject should be indifferent in his choice between obtaining B for sure and the lottery in which A occurs as the prize with probability .69 and E is the prize with probability .31. Similarly, the subject should be indifferent between object D for sure and the lottery in which A is the prize with probability .154 and E is the prize with probability .846. These p values form an interval scale of utility. They differ from the true values only by a multiplicative and an additive constant.

This potential method for measuring utility or personal value is presented as another excellent example of the dependence of a scaling method on a theory of human behavior. The theory here rests on two basic assumptions: Preference behavior is directly related to utility value with indifference in preference indicating equality of utility. Also, the utility of a lottery is simply the expected utility of its prizes. If this theory is true, it follows that preferences among lotteries provide an interval scale of utility.

It should be perfectly obvious, of course, that any attempt to measure utility for other than a very small number of objects would be both time-consuming and fraught with all sorts of procedural and experimental hazards. For example, seldom would a subject submit to the comparison of a large number of lotteries without becoming genuinely indifferent or hostile to the whole experimental enterprise. Nevertheless, the method does have some direct use in the experimental psychology of value, and it also serves as a point of departure for more sophisticated and practicable methods. Here, as elsewhere, given the complete theoretical substructure, the technique of measurement emerges as a simple consequence.

RATING SCALES

One of the simplest and most used of the devices for psychological measurement is the numerical rating scale. The rater is simply given a set of ordered categories or intervals, each associated with a numerical rating, and is asked to place the object of judgment in the most appropriate category or at the most appropriate point on a graphic scale. His rating is then taken to indicate the amount of the psychological characteristic he perceives in the object. Thus, for example, the quality of organizing ability is to be rated. The rater may be given a graphic scale consisting of a straight line marked off into seven equal intervals. On the boundaries between the intervals may appear the numbers 1 through 6. Then any given object of judgment, such as another person, is placed at the appropriate point along the line. Most often, the number nearest to the position assigned to the object is taken as the score or rating.

Sometimes the rater is simply presented with such a scale, and his ratings are treated as the amounts of the psychological characteristic shown by the objects. Then the implicit assumption is made that the rater is somehow able to translate his perception of the object directly into a number. Although this assumption is frequently made, it is, nevertheless, a rather strong assumption in most instances. In particular, the assumption that a difference between ratings in the middle portion of the scale is psychologically equivalent to the same numerical difference in ratings near either extreme of the scale often contradicts both intuition and the available evidence.

On the other hand, numerical ratings can also be interpreted only as *ordinal* indicators of the true perceived positions of the objects. This is a considerably weaker assumption than before, of course, as it does not imply anything at all about the meaning of differences in numerical ratings. However, when ratings are treated only as ordinal measurements, the statistical treatment of rating data becomes more difficult, at least in terms of application of the more powerful statistical methods. The psychologist may then feel that he is not making full use of the information provided by the raters. For this reason, although raw ratings are often treated as measurement values just as they stand, the psychologist may wish to convert the raw ratings into other values by making one or more theoretical assumptions.

One of the oldest and simplest assumptions made in collecting and analyzing rating data is that of *equal-appearing intervals*. The rater is told explicitly that the intervals into which the rating scale is divided should be *psychologically equal*. That is, the rater is to adopt the attitude that an object rated exactly 1 is psychologically just as different from an object rated 2 as the object with rating 2 is from an object rated 3. The assumption is that the rater can indeed hold this instructional set in mind and can assign objects accordingly. In assigning any given object along the scale, the rater is presumed to compare the perceived status of the object to the idealized values represented by the boundaries of the equal intervals. Furthermore, it is assumed that if variability occurs among the ratings of a given object across a group of judges, this variability reflects disagreements about the status of the object but does not reflect any disagreement about the boundaries of the intervals into which objects may fall. Then, a *median* position may be found for any given object across the judges, and this is treated as its true position.

Consider the following example of data collected on a graphic rating scale, divided into equal-appearing intervals:

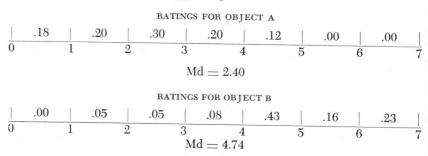

RATINGS FOR OBJECT A

	.18		.20		.30		.20		.12		.00		.00	
0		1		2		3		4		5		6		7

Md = 2.40

RATINGS FOR OBJECT B

	.00		.05		.05		.08		.43		.16		.23	
0		1		2		3		4		5		6		7

Md = 4.74

In this rating scale, there are seven intervals and thus six boundaries between intervals. The number within any given interval on the first scale shows the proportional number of times object A was rated within that interval. The second scale also shows the same equal divisions, but this time the proportions correspond to ratings of object B. Assigning a scale value to object A, then, amounts simply to finding the median value of A as distributed over the equal intervals. Exactly .38 of the total distribution of A judgments fall at or below the category boundary 2, while .68 fall at or below category boundary 3. If one can assume a *uniform* spread of values within categories, the value of the median must be $(.50 -.38)/.30$ of the interval above the value 2, or

$$\text{median value for } A = 2 + (.50 -.38)/.30 = 2.40.$$

Similarly, the median value for B is found from:

$$\text{median value for } B = 4 + (.50 -.18)/.43 = 4.74.$$

In the same way the median value can be found for any other object rated. These median values are best estimates of A, B, and so forth, in the sense that they are closest, on the average, to the ratings of the individual judges—provided, of course, that the intervals used by each judge are truly equal in psychological value.

Quite often one wishes to construct a rating scale in which *marker* stimuli represent different psychological values. These marker stimuli illustrate increasing degrees of a trait. The rater who applies the scale to a new object of judgment can place a new stimulus in the appropriate interval between the markers and thus assign it an approximate value. For example, we might wish to characterize any American political figure on a dimension of liberalism versus conservatism. First, a relatively large and heterogeneous group of well-known political figures are taken as the initial set of stimuli. Then, each of these stimuli is given to a large group of judges who rate each stimulus on an equal appearing interval scale. The data for five such stimuli might appear as in Table 8.

Here, once again, the proportion of judges rating the stimuli in an interval is shown. Then, just as before, the median value for each stimulus object can be computed. From these stimulus values a smaller set of stimuli is taken. In the smaller set (1) the stimuli successively differ from each other by about the same amount, (2) as wide a range of values as possible is included, and (3) the variability shown by each stimulus is as small as possible. In the example stimulus A has the value 1.29, B the value 5.00, C the value 5.00, D the value 2.32, and E the value 3.87. Thus, these stimulus objects can be thought of as spread fairly evenly across the scale, with the exception of B and C, which show the same median value.

Which of the two stimulus objects B and C should be used as marker points for the final scale? The answer is one of variability.

Table 8

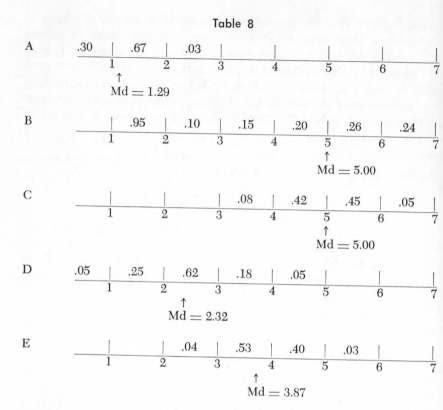

The stimuli chosen as markers for a scale should show the smallest possible variance over the judges. It is obvious that the judges spread their ratings over a larger range of intervals for B than for C, meaning that there was greater variance of ratings and hence less agreement about the position of B than about the position of C. Therefore, the less variable stimulus, C, is chosen. (Note that one can actually compute variances of ratings by regarding each set of ratings for a stimulus as a grouped frequency distribution.)

Finally, we have a new rating scale, in which *marker stimuli* appear. A rater using this new scale has only to decide where any new stimulus falls among the marker stimuli provided. If the new stimulus, say F, falls between A and B, then its value is between 1.29 and 2.32. If F falls between E and C, its value is between 3.87 and 5. Given such a rating scale with marker stimuli, values (or at least intervals of values) can be given to any new stimulus object as desired. Each new stimulus is evaluated with respect to positions already accorded the original marker stimuli. One very popular application of this method in the past has been in the construction of attitude scales. Some uses of attitude scales will be discussed in a subsequent section.

Rating-scale methods can also be thought of as variants of successive intervals methods. Indeed, whenever the subject must place stimulus objects into any set of ordered categories that represent degrees of some continuous characteristic, he simply sorts the items into successive intervals. This implies that numerical interval-scale values can also be obtained from ratings scales by adopting assumptions other than equal-appearing intervals. In particular, the assumption of a normal distribution of ratings can be used to find scale values.

Suppose that seven categories or intervals are used on a rating scale and that each subject rates *himself* (or perhaps one other individual, such as his father) on some characteristic. This implies, of course, that there should be exactly as many ratings as subjects. We wish to assign scale values to the subjects in terms of their self-ratings on this characteristic. The pooled data across s jects might appear as in Table 9, which shows the cumulative proportion at or below each of the category boundaries.

In treating such data, first one may assume that the distribution of values across subjects *should* be normal in form with some mean, μ, and some variance, σ^2. Then one uses the method of finding *mean category values* already given above under methods for successive intervals judgments. That is, the mean for the lowest category is found from:

$$\text{category mean} = \frac{(\text{density at lower limit}) - (\text{density at upper limit})}{(\text{proportion below upper limit}) - (\text{proportion below lower limit})}$$

$$= \frac{0 - .0264}{.01 - 0} = -2.64.$$

In Table 9 exactly 1 percent of the individuals judged themselves at or below the first category boundary. This category boundary corresponds, in a normal distribution, to a z value of -2.33 and an ordinate or density value of .0264. The hypothetical lower limit to this interval would have a z score of minus infinity and a density value of 0. Hence, one finds that the mean of this first interval in z score terms is -2.64.

In this same way, just as in the successive intervals example already given, the mean value for each of the remaining categories is found. These category means are shown in Table 9. Then each of the self-ratings by subjects is given the value of the mean of the category in which it falls. Thus, a subject rating himself as falling into the second category gets a value of —1.99. Notice that the mean value of any category and hence the value for any subject placing himself in that category now is relative to the entire distribution of subjects' ratings over categories. If a category is both extreme and rarely used, this category gets a higher absolute value than if the category is relatively frequently used. Witness the first and the last categories in this example.

This method is quite useful when subjects rate themselves on a

Table 9

Cumulative proportions of self-ratings by categories, and category mean values.

	1	2	3	4	5	6	7
CUMULATIVE PROPORTIONS	.01	.04	.08	.28	.61	.91	1.00
MEAN CATEGORY VALUES	−2.64	−1.99	−1.53	−.948	.080	.736	1.87

variety of psychological traits or characteristics and one wishes to compare the ratings of a subject across these traits. In this procedure, one scales *as though* the true values for subjects on any given trait were normally distributed with a mean of zero and a variance of 1.00. In addition, one assumes implicitly that the values represented by the category boundaries are *constant* for each of the subjects.

It should also be pointed out that when a number of stimulus objects are being rated by a sizable group of judges, the data may be converted into numerical values by the Law of Categorical Judgment procedure discussed above. Here, of course, it is not necessary to assume that the category boundaries are constant across judges; but it is necessary to assume both that the values for any object across judges and the boundary values perceived by the judges are normally distributed. In situations where the status of an object of judgment is to be examined across several traits or rated characteristics, this may be the best method to use. The objects are, of course, rated on each trait separately by the judges, and then the scale values are found separately for each trait. Such scale values may then be compared or correlated across the traits for any object.

A great deal of study has been devoted to the advantages and disadvantages of rating methods as applied to psychological characteristics. Although it is the simplest appearing of all of the methods for psychological measurement, there are a great many pitfalls to be avoided in the application of rating scales. Space and the level of discussion here do not permit us to go into these precautions, but a discussion such as that in Guilford (1954, Chapter 11) can be read with profit by anyone contemplating the use of rating devices.

EXERCISES AND PROBLEMS

1. Aside from those in the text, give additional examples of:
   a. Three physical properties of living things that can be measured more or less directly.
   b. Three implicit or latent properties of living things that can be measured only indirectly.
2. Suppose that workers in a vegetable canning factory must sort cut green beans according to length. You wish to evaluate individual workers on their ability to spot beans that vary only slightly in size. Would you say this is a problem in psychophysics or in psychometrics? Why?
3. Seventy-five percent of the time a worker in a canning factory can tell when a cut green bean is 1/16 inch or more longer than the standard size of exactly 1 inch. If $S_0 = 1$ inch, then what is the value of $S = S_0 + \triangle S$?
4. In experiments on judgments of elapsed time, it is found that people ordinarily can easily tell the difference between 30 seconds and a minute. However, they have more difficulty detecting the difference between a minute and a minute and one half. What principle of psychophysics might this illustrate?
5. In an experiment, subjects judged the frequency with which a very fast metronome was ticking. They did this by actually moving a dial to the numerical setting they thought represented the rate. Would this experiment more likely represent the Stevens or the Weber-Fechner approach to psychophysics? Why?
6. Make up at least three examples, other than those given in the text, in which psychological scaling might be carried out for a nonphysical property.
7. Six small objects were judged for size by a large number of judges through pair comparisons. The data produced by this experiment are as follows and are stated in terms of the number of times that the column of objects was judged heavier than that in the row:

	A	B	C	D	E	F
A	.50	.81	.83	.84	.90	.45
B	.19	.50	.52	.55	.88	.31
C	.17	.48	.50	.54	.75	.29
D	.16	.45	.46	.50	.73	.25
E	.10	.12	.25	.27	.50	.08
F	.55	.69	.71	.75	.92	.50

Complete the scaling of these objects by the Thurstone Law of Comparative Judgment method.

8. Can you see any way that the Thurstone method might possibly be checked by going from the scale values *back* to the table of pair-comparison proportions? Describe how this might be done.

9. Before the start of the season, forty-one baseball writers ranked ten American League teams as shown in the following table:

Rank

		1	2	3	4	5	6	7	8	9	10
	A	16	8	0	17	0	0	0	0	0	0
	B	7	10	0	7	17	0	0	0	0	0
	C	0	17	10	7	1	0	0	0	0	6
	D	17	0	14	10	0	0	0	0	0	0
TEAM	E	1	0	17	0	23	0	0	0	0	0
	F	0	6	0	0	0	34	0	0	1	0
	G	0	0	0	0	0	1	10	23	0	7
	H	0	0	0	0	0	0	31	10	0	0
	I	0	0	0	0	0	0	0	0	40	1
	J	0	0	0	0	0	6	0	8	0	27

From this table of rankings, scale the projected "ability" of the ten teams. How would you describe the writers' ability to judge among A, B, C, and D, as opposed to F, G, H, and I? How is this reflected on the final scale?

10. A mail-order company was considering marketing a new line of household utensils. It asked a large sample of women to judge a number of these household utensils according to "practicality". Seven categories of judgment were permitted, ranging from "not practical at all" (1) to "extremely practical" (7). The results follow, showing the proportion of judgments in each category:

.09	.02	.04	.20	.43	.12	.10
1	2	3	4	5	6	7

Scale these categories to find their boundary and mean values. What value in practicality would a utensil get if it were rated by all of the women to be in category 7? Is a utensil in category 5 to be regarded as *much inferior* to a utensil in category 6, if category 7 is used as the standard?

11. Four lecturers are rated for effectiveness of teaching by a group of several hundred students. Seven categories, ranging from "very poor" (1) to "superlative" (7), were used. The data below show the proportion of ratings at or below each category boundary for each instructor:

CATEGORY BOUNDARY

LECTURER	(1,2)	(2,3)	(3,4)	(4,5)	(5,6)	(6,7)
A	.00	.12	.34	.53	.69	.90
B	.10	.40	.59	.78	.93	.97
C	.02	.04	.30	.51	.75	.98
D	.20	.47	.66	.81	.87	.96

Scale both the category boundaries and the effectiveness of the four teachers as rated by the students.

12. A student stated that in a given course he would be exactly indifferent to receiving a B grade for sure or to flipping a coin with the instructor to see whether he got an A or a C. Scale the utility of A, B, and C for that student. Suppose he was indifferent between B for sure or drawing a *heart* from a deck of cards to get an A— otherwise a C. In that case, does the scaling show that an A is relatively more or less valuable to the student than before?

13. Scale the instructors from the data in problem 11 above. Assume that the students had been informed they were to use the method of equal-appearing intervals.

The devices for psychological measurement discussed previously are designed for scaling stimulus values, either in terms of a known or an assumed connection between physical values and psychological counterparts (psychophysics) or in terms of implicit differences between the stimuli as seen by one or more judges (as in Thurstone scaling). In each instance, the end product was a value assigned to each stimulus object. The value presumably reflected the magnitude or amount shown by that object on the psychological characteristic in question. As has been seen, one's ability to attach numerical values to the stimulus objects may come from the assumption that a particular form of relation holds between a physical property and the behavior of a judge (as in psychophysical methods). Or scale values may rest on the assumption that differences in behaviors with respect to stimuli are related to the psychological values of the stimuli in some specific way (as in utility measurement) or that the statistical distribution of perceived values of a stimulus follows a known form (as in Thurstone scaling and its variants). In all instances, however, the subject is given the task of telling something about the stimuli and their relations to each other. He is asked if stimulus A is brighter than stimulus B or to rank people according to leadership ability. He is asked to classify statements among categories of liberalism-conservatism. In another instance he may be asked if he would rather have this object for sure or participate in this lottery. The emphasis in every case is on *perceived differences* among the stimulus objects and not on the subjects themselves and the possible differences among them.

A very large part of traditional psychological measurement involves assessment of the amount of some psychological trait or ability shown by the subject himself. The main goal is not to obtain values that are characteristic of each of a set of varying stimuli in the presence of a constant subject. Rather, the main goal is to find values characteristic of each of a set of subjects as inferred by their behaviors in the presence of some constant stimulus situation. The subject is assumed to possess a certain amount of intelligence, or degree of mechanical skill, or favorableness of attitude toward a particular institution, or level of anxiety. A numerical value is to be assigned to *him* rather than to any external stimulus. The branch of psychological measurement concerned with the assessment of the status of an individual himself on a psychological trait is usually called *psychometrics*, as distinct from psychophysics or stimulus scaling. There is, however, an enormous overlap between the methods of psychometrics and those used for scaling stimuli. And almost any of the stimulus-scaling methods can, in principle, be used for the comparison of individual subjects. Indeed, any technique may be used to scale stimuli or to scale subjects. This is largely a matter of emphasis, either on what is varied or on what is held constant in the data-gathering situation.

DIRECT AND INDIRECT MEASUREMENT
BASED ON BEHAVIORS

As has been noted, there are many quite obvious, direct, and to the point ways to measure stimulus objects or to measure people. Such techniques involve nothing that is peculiar to psychological scaling and they can be applied without elaborate scaling procedures. Perhaps it is well to emphasize this point once again in connection with the measurement of subjects. Clearly, at any moment in time each subject will have some status on a variety of physical properties, such as height, weight, age, body temperature, or the volume of excreted urea. The subject may be measured on these properties with only the most passive participation on his part. Furthermore, voluntary or involuntary behaviors of the subject may also be measured in physical terms. We may find out his heart rate, for example, or his chest expansion or the strength of grip in his right hand. In addition, one may choose to count the number of times that the subject performs a given behavior in a given situation in a given time period—the number of push-ups he is able to do without stopping or the number of words he can recall from a list.

Generally, of most interest and importance to psychologists are measurements based upon some voluntary or involuntary behavior of the subject in the presence of one or more stimuli. The subject is an active participant in the measurement process. In some instances, the interest of the psychologist stops with the simple occurrence or non-occurrence of a given behavior. For example, does or does not an infant show a particular reflex when the sole of his foot is stroked? Does or does not the child turn right in a given portion of a maze? On the other hand, the psychologist may wish to go further and to infer the amount of some psychological characteristic of the subject, basing this inference on one or more behaviors of the subject. Here it is not the behavior itself that is of primary interest but rather the psychological state that lies behind the behavior. The behaviors that occur are thought of as signaling the kind and degree of the psychological situation going on within the person. The recording of behaviors of an individual may be a fairly simple process; inferring the meaning of those behaviors, as they refer to some psychological characteristic, may be difficult in the extreme. Certainly, such an inference requires a rationale—a logical connection between the behaviors actually observed and the psychological situation they presumably reflect. In the preceding chapter, we saw that there are various possible theoretical links between behaviors of one or more subjects and between the presumed psychological magnitudes of one or more stimulus objects. The same is true for scaling individual subjects on psychological properties. One must have a rationale for going from behaviors to the subject's status on a psychological characteristic.

Although the more direct measurement of physical properties of a subject, including direct counts or physical measures of his behaviors, are extremely important in psychology, the methods to be dealt with here will be confined to ones that measure the implicit psychological characteristics that can be inferred and measured only indirectly. Such psychological concepts as strength of attitude, general intelligence, special aptitudes, motives, and emotional states cannot usually be measured simply from isolated behaviors. Rather, they are measured by inference from whole patterns of behavior in the presence of a standard set of stimuli. These are the kinds of psychological characteristics, measured indirectly, of concern here.

MENTAL TESTS

The most characteristic tool of psychometrics is the mental test. Particular mental tests and their use in the study of individual differences and personality assessment are discussed in another volume in this series, and so we will not treat the subject very deeply or extensively here. However, a few of the basic features of the theory of mental tests will be mentioned.

For our purposes a mental test may be defined as *a standard stimulus situation to which a person responds in such a way as to produce one or more scores that reflect his own status on one or more psychological characteristics.* A familiar example of a mental test is a pencil and paper intelligence test. Every modern American school child has encountered such a test in one form or another. Here, the standard stimulus situation consists of the items on the test itself together with the standardized setting in which it is administered. The responses to the situation are the subject's answers to the test questions. The score on the test, ordinarily based on the number and type of questions answered correctly within certain time limits, is then translated into another score, the intelligence quotient. This last value, the intelligence quotient, presumably tells the status of the individual subject on a psychological, implicit, characteristic: general intelligence. Other familiar examples that have much the same format are achievement tests, aptitude tests, interest tests, attitude tests, and various types of personality tests. Ordinarily, when a person speaks of psychological tests, he means one of these types of standardized mental tests.

STANDARDIZED TESTS

By far the majority of mental tests are standardized tests. This term, standardized, means that the score of the individual subject is compared and interpreted in the light of the scores of a large number of individuals of some known group who have also taken the test. Thus, for example, the commonly encountered intelligence tests are accompanied by extensive tables that show the distributions of scores obtained by individuals of various ages. If an individual obtains a score that is unusually high for individuals of his age group, then he receives a high intelligence quotient. If, on the other hand, his score is unusually low for comparable subjects, he receives a low intelligence quotient. The point is that in a standardized test, the individual is evaluated in comparison to a standard group of subjects who have been given the same test.

The same idea applies to other than intelligence tests. For example, in a test of musical aptitude, the score of the individual may serve to place him among a set of subjects known to have, or not to have, musical ability. In an interest test, the pattern of responses of the individual will be compared with the pattern shown by a number of known interest and occupational groups. In a personality test, the pattern of responses of the subject may be compared with those of a number of groups known to show particular personality traits in some extreme degree. In each instance, the score or pattern of scores of the individual is interpreted in the light of the scores of patterns obtained from standard comparison groups.

Obviously, all tests need not be standardized. Certain personality tests are interpreted not by comparison with a standard comparison group but are interpreted separately as a reflection of the individual's own personality dynamics. In some tests of achievement, the individual may be compared with himself over time. Nevertheless, the standardized test is by far the most common variety of psychological test. And in this discussion of mental tests, except when noted to the contrary, the reference is to standardized tests.

SPEED AND POWER TESTS

Characteristically, a mental test consists of a number of items, each of which demands a behavioral response from the subject. On a test of arithmetic ability, for example, the subject is asked, "How much is 81 divided by 3?" He responds to this item. And his answer qualifies as either a pass or a fail. On a personality test, the subject may be asked whether or not he dreads meeting new people. Here, too, his answer may be translated into pass or fail or into positive versus negative. Each item on a mental test may be likened to a hurdle on a racing track. The test item is like a hurdle placed before the subject, and his response is analogous to his clearing or not clearing the hurdle. Carrying the analogy still further, the hurdles on a track may be of two kinds, either all of the same height, or of increasing height. A race over the hurdles may be thought of as a test of "hurdling" ability; if the contestant clears all of the hurdles placed before him, without regard to speed, his ability may properly be thought of as at least as great as that required by the highest hurdle. John Doe clears a hurdle 6 feet tall, and hence he can be said to have hurdling ability greater than that required by 6 feet. Richard Roe, on the other hand, can clear 5 feet 5 inches, but not 6 feet; thus, we can say that his hurdling ability is less than John Doe's and also that it is less than that required by 6 feet but greater than 5 feet 5 inches. Presumably, there is some hurdle height which would *exactly* match each boy's ability.

This analogy of a mental test to a hurdle race is not altogether bad. A so-called *power test* consists of a set of items *graded* or *stepped* in terms of their *difficulty*. Thus, there are relatively low-hurdle items, some of medium difficulty, and still others of relatively great difficulty. Presumably, the ability of the person taking the test should be reflected by the maximum difficulty of the items he is able to pass. If numerical values, representing difficulty, and thus amounts of required ability, are attached to the items, the person can be given a value in terms of the items passed and those failed. A great many tests of ability are of this type, where the items have been evaluated for difficulty, and the score of the individual is found from the value or the average value attached to the passed items. Most attitude tests are also of this form. As we have seen, attitude statements can be scaled or evaluated according to the degree of favorableness or unfavorableness they represent. Then the respondent's own attitude position is inferred to be above the value of items that he can endorse but below the value of items that he fails to endorse. Personality tests as well may have the form of a power test. Certain behaviors or feelings may represent very mild degrees of some psychological trait whereas others represent that trait in moderate or extreme degree. By endorsing items as true or false when applied to himself, the person evaluates himself with respect to the trait.

Let us resume the hurdle analogy once again, however. Most such races involve many hurdles of the same height, and the ability of an individual is inferred from the time taken to clear all of the hurdles. One might also score such a race from the number of hurdles of the same height a contestant clears in a fixed amount of time. Many mental tests parallel this form of race, since they consist of many items, each of equivalent difficulty and presumably requiring the same amount of skill. Here the score given the individual is based on the time he takes to complete all of the items or on the number of items he is able to complete in a fixed amount of time. Such tests are called *pure speed tests*, to distinguish them from power tests. Presumably, the person who successfully completes only 25 items on such a test is indicating that he has less of the ability required than a person who completes 100 such items in the same time.

Most mental tests combine both speed and power features. On any test item, however, the respondent can be thought of as comparing his own amount of ability or degree of a trait against the amount or degree required by the item. Particularly in power tests, the essential problem in test construction is the selection and evaluation of items which actually do require successively increasing amounts of the ability or trait to be measured.

DIFFICULTY, HOMOGENEITY, AND INTERNAL CONSISTENCY

If we were setting out to construct a pure speed test of arithmetic ability, we would first of all like to choose a set of items each of which required the same amount of ability on the part of the subject. Suppose that the test were being constructed for children of third-grade level. Then we would like items that were of equal difficulty for a group of such children. A large pool of items would be given to a sizable group of third graders. Then, items that the same proportion of children passed could be selected. For example, we might select those items that 75 percent of children passed and 25 percent of the children in the group failed.

However, something else is required. How does one know that the items are not passed or failed for different reasons? Can one assure himself that all of the items reflect arithmetic ability? It is possible, for example, to throw in an item on spelling that 75 percent of the children might pass. But, clearly, this does not appear to have much to do with arithmetic ability. What is needed is a set of *homogeneous* items, items that do give evidence of measuring the same thing. If two items are homogeneous, then a child who fails one will tend to fail the other, and if he passes one, he will tend to pass the other.

Homogeneous items are *highly correlated* items. If items are more or less pure reflections of a given trait or ability, then they should tend to correlate highly. The most usual measure of the correlation of test items—and thus an index of their homogeneity—is the phi coefficient (introduced in *Basic Statistics* in this series).

The *difficulty* of an item is, of course, always relative to the performance of some group. The simplest indicator of difficulty is the proportion of individuals failing to pass the item. Thus, an item with difficulty 1.00 would be passed by none of the persons attempting it, and an item with difficulty 0 would be passed by all who attempt it. In some instances, item difficulties are converted to z values corresponding to the proportion of area under a normal curve equivalent to the proportion failing an item. The z value is called the index of difficulty. Thus, for example, if 75 percent of persons fail a particular test item, this would give a difficulty index of .68, since 75 per cent of the area under a normal curve is cut off by a z value of .68.

On the other hand, suppose that we wanted to construct a pure power test of arithmetic ability, again for third-grade-level children. Now we no longer wish to have all items of equal difficulty, as represented in our group of subjects. Rather, we desire a range of items, from very easy to very difficult for our group of third-graders. Thus, from an initial large pool of possible items, we select such a range of easy to difficult, depending on how many of our standard group of third grade children manage to pass each one. However, is our job then done? How do we know that each one of the items selected for the power test really measures arithmetic ability? Perhaps the very easy items measure one thing and the difficult items measure another. One clue that we are indeed measuring the same characteristic throughout comes from the *internal consistency* of the items. Consider three arithmetic items, A, which is apparently very easy, B which is moderately difficult, and C, which is much more difficult than B. Now if A, B, and C were perfectly consistent, an individual who can pass C should be able to pass A and B. Furthermore, an individual who can pass B but who fails C should still pass A. If an individual fails A, he should pass *neither* B nor C. In short, items of increasing difficulty can be examined for this kind of internal consistency, and the most consistent set of items taken as the basis for the power test. Note that unlike a pure speed test, which assumes homogeneous items, and thus highly correlated items, the items on a power test should be internally consistent but *not necessarily* highly correlated.

THEORETICALLY AND EMPIRICALLY BASED TESTS

Traditionally, tests are classified as *theoretically based* or *empirically based*. In the first instance the items are selected and weighted primarily on the basis of some theoretical connection with the trait or ability to be measured. In the second, the items are selected and weighted primarily in terms of their statistical relation to one or more practical distinctions. For example, if we wished to construct a test of managerial ability, there are certainly at least two ways of proceeding. We might first list all of the qualities that, in theory, should and should not be possessed by a good manager or all of the specific behaviors that he should or should not exhibit. We might well submit the list to a panel of managerial experts, who, by their agreements or disagreements on specific terms, would be asked to select a set of items that seem most relevant. We might even go further and have the expert judges carry out pair comparisons among the items or make successive intervals judgments. The results would make it possible to scale the items by methods such as those given above. Then, a score could be given to the subject taking the test. The score could be found perhaps by taking the mean of the values of items that he passed or endorsed. Such a test would be largely theoretically based, since the item selection and evaluation is carried out exclusively in terms of theoretical notions or expert judgment about the characteristics that should or should not be true of a good manager.

The second way of proceeding would be to begin by finding two groups of persons. One group would be made up of men who are, by general consensus, good managers. The other group would be made up of poor managers. A large heterogeneous set of items could be given to each member of each of the two groups, and the items themselves could then be evaluated according to the extent that one group responds positively to the item and the other group responds negatively. Having found a fairly small set of *discriminating items* one would proceed to construct the test from this set, perhaps weighting the items according to the extent to which each did discriminate the good managers from the poor. The score of a subject taking the test would then be the weighted sum of the items answered in the positive (good manager) direction. Here, there is no requirement that an item appear on the surface to have anything at all to do with managerial ability. Indeed, there are some advantages to having the items seem very remote from the trait measured, particularly if one fears that respondents might wish to fake the test to their own advantage. An item such as "Do you like hard-centered or soft-centered chocolates?" might well differentiate the two groups very well. All that is required is that the items, whatever they may be, do consistently discriminate between the responses of good and bad managers. Such a test would be empirically, rather than theoretically, based.

Elements of both empirical and theoretical item selection go into the makeup of most psychological tests. Naturally, however, the details of item selection and evaluation differ widely, depending on how much is known, theoretically and empirically, about the trait to be measured. Generally, the analysis of the items composing any test is concerned with two issues: the *validity* of the item, meaning the extent to which the item does indeed measure the psychological property intended, and the *difficulty*, or *weight*, of the item, meaning *how much* of the property under study actually seems to be reflected in the successful performance of the item. The validity of an item is ideally assessed by the relation of that item to some *criterion*, such as two groups known to be extremely different on the trait being measured. An item is considered valid to the extent that large differences in performance on the item exist between members of different criterion groups. An item is also considered valid to the extent that individuals who show different performance on it also show consistent differences on one or more other measures of the same trait. The validity of an item may even be assessed in terms of the extent to which it is related to all of the remaining items on the test. As has been shown, a test in which performance on any single item is predictive of the performance on any other item is said to *homogeneous*. Presumably, all items in a homogeneous test measure the same trait, and homogeneity may thus indicate one aspect of test validity.

RELIABILITY AND VALIDITY

Regardless of the manner in which test items are selected, however, any mental test is subject to a certain degree of *unreliability*. That is, the value assigned to an individual on the basis of his performance on the test will tend to vary, depending on the particular occasion on which the test was administered. Naturally, there is always a chance or accidental component to the performance of an individual on a test. Many events, such as how the subject happens to feel at the particular time of taking the test, the distractions that occur, any unfortunate lapse of attention, and lucky and unlucky guesses, have an influence on a person's score. Such chance occurrences really do not reflect his true ability or status on the psychological trait; but they can and do influence the subject's score. Tests differ in the extent to which the scores they provide are prone to such chance *errors of measurement* and in the usual magnitude of such errors. The *true score* of any individual on a test may be thought of as his typical or average score over all possible occasions; but his *obtained score* on any *given* occasion consists of that true score (T) plus some error component (e). Thus if X is the score obtained on any given testing occasion,

$$X = T + e.$$

Over all possible occasions, the chance or error portions, e, are assumed to have a distribution of values with a mean of zero but with some variance σ_e^2. To the extent that the error variance is small the test tends to be reliable; but to the extent that the error variance is large, the test tends to be unreliable. In particular, if the error variance σ_e^2 is the same for any individual as for any other and if σ_T^2 is the variance of the true values across individuals, then

$$\text{reliability of the test} = \frac{\sigma_T^2}{\sigma_T^2 + \sigma_e^2}$$

or

$$\text{unreliability of the test} = \frac{\sigma_e^2}{\sigma_T^2 + \sigma_e^2}$$

In other words, the total variability $(\sigma_T^2 + \sigma_e^2)$ among scores for any group of individuals on a test must be due to two things: true differences among the individuals, as reflected in the value of σ_T^2, and error variability, as reflected in the value of σ_e^2. Hence, *the reliability of a test can be defined as the proportion of the total variability among scores due to the true differences among individuals.* Similarly, *the unreliability of a test is defined as the proportion of the total observed variability due to errors in measurement.* A very elaborate theory of mental tests exists, which is centered around the problem of test reliability and of experimental methods for determining test reliability. This definition of test reliability is the basis for the theory of mental tests.

Hand in hand with the problem of the reliability of a test goes the question of its *validity*. Essentially, when we ask about the validity of a test, we are inquiring "To what extent does the test actually measure the ability or trait it was designed to measure?" This usually boils down to the question "Do the scores on this test predict the things that they should predict, and fail to predict those things irrelevant to the ability or trait under study?" If a test is designed to measure managerial ability, then it should predict the behaviors that are dependent on managerial ability. If the test is designed to measure general intelligence, then high scores on this test should predict intelligent performances in other contexts, and low scores should predict less intelligent performances. Thus, the *predictive validity* of a test is the most usual meaning of the term "validity."

However, it is sometimes not possible to find a clear criterion behavior which the test should predict. Clear-cut evidence for the predictive validity of a test may thus be very hard to obtain. In such instances, the validity of a test may be inferred from the extent to which its scores predict those of still another test designed to measure the same, or a very similar, psychological characteristic. This is called the argument for the *concurrent validity* of a test. For example, a great many forms of intelligence tests claim their validity because they predict scores on other well-established tests of intelligence.

In still other instances, tests are claimed to be valid because of some strong theoretical argument why they *should* measure whatever is claimed. Such arguments usually assert that items such as those on the test, and only such items, tap the psychological trait or ability in question. Such arguments for *construct validity*, unaccompanied by supporting evidence for predictive or for concurrent validity, are fortunately rather rare, but they are occasionally recognized as appropriate ways of justifying a particular form of tests. The early projective tests of personality were often defended in this way. In any case, anyone constructing a mental test must make some plausible argument and, hopefully, present convincing evidence that the test is valid or measures whatever is claimed for it.

The student is referred to a companion volume in this series on the assessment of human characteristics for a more detailed discussion of mental tests and to any of a number of good texts on psychological tests and measurement, such as Anastasi (1956), Tyler (1956), or Cronbach (1960). Suffice it to say here that a mental test differs essentially from any other psychological measurement techniques in that the individual, by his behavior toward some constant set of stimuli, is regarded as placing *himself* along some psychological attribute or continuum. The items that make up a test are stimuli designed to evoke the appropriate behaviors, and they permit one to attach a numerical value to a person's performance as a whole. The details of test construction and of test theory provide guides for choosing and weighting the item stimuli and for evaluating the reliability and validity of the resultant scores.

ATTITUDE MEASUREMENT

In the last fifty years, American psychologists and sociologists have devoted a great deal of attention to the concept of attitude. Attitudes have been defined in various ways. In one conventional definition an attitude is "a more or less enduring predisposition to respond affectively toward a specified entity" (Jahoda *et al.*, 1951, p. 112). Put more simply, an individual is thought of as having a tendency to respond positively or negatively to a specific situation, person, or thing. This positive or negative tendency can be strong or weak and can exist at the same level over fairly long periods of time. In many areas of study it is important to try to get at attitudes of people and to attempt to measure them.

Attitude measurement gives one of the clearest examples of the thin line that exists between stimulus scaling methods and measurement techniques for the individual subject. Indeed, the Thurstone techniques for stimulus scaling have been used most widely in the construction of attitude scales.

The typical attitude scale or attitude test resembles a power test. That is, a series of statements concerning some situation or entity is given to the subject. His task is to respond by agreeing or disagreeing with (endorsing or not endorsing) each statement. For example, an item on attitude toward household pets might read:

Dogs and cats by their habits are unsanitary and should not be allowed within a household. (Agree, Disagree)

A whole series of such statements is given to the subject. Some of the statements are positive in the direction of the attitude represented, and others are less positive or negative. Each statement, however, is assigned a value that represents the amount of favorableness (or unfavorableness) of attitude an endorsement of the statement should represent. After the person responds to each statement and attitude, a score may be found for him either by taking the values of all of the endorsed items or, in some cases, by taking the value of the most extreme statement endorsed.

The similarity of such a test of attitude to a power test is shown in at least two ways. In the first place, the attitude items must be scaled in some way and given values much as the items on a power test are scaled in terms of their difficulty. Second, the items on an attitude scale should tend to be internally consistent if one is to be confident that a single unitary attitude is being tapped. Thus, ideally, a person's responses to the attitude statements should be consistent at least in the sense that if one extremely positive statement is endorsed other statements in the same extreme direction should be endorsed.

The Thurstone method of pair comparisons and the Law of Comparative Judgment scaling method can be applied directly to the construction of an attitude scale. A group of judges is given pairs of statements and is asked to judge which of the statements is the more positive with respect to the attitude in question. Then, the scaling method previously outlined is applied. This results in a set of items that have a relatively equal distribution from unfavorable to favorable and can be given to subjects for individual response. Generally, the average scale value of statements endorsed by the subject is taken as his score on the attitude in question.

Pair comparison methods, however, are quite laborious to carry out, and it is far more usual to find the method of successive intervals, or of equal appearing intervals, used for this purpose. The scaling procedure in either case proceeds exactly as is described in the preceding sections, except that here each stimulus is an attitude statement. Then, a set of widely differing items is selected from among those scaled, and these are the items given to the subjects. In scoring the subject, one uses the scale values of the items endorsed.

Quite a different approach to the construction of an attitude scale for administration to individual subjects is that originally developed by Louis Guttman. This approach has become known as *scalogram analysis*. Guttman's method emphasizes internal consistency as evidence that the different items do represent different quantitative positions on the same basic dimension. For example, consider three items:

A. Students should have some voice in university policy. (Agree, Disagree)

B. Students should be consulted on matters such as curriculum changes. (Agree, Disagree)

C. Student representatives should sit with the Board of Regents in decisions affecting all university policy. (Agree, Disagree)

Now, in the following diagram, consider the answers of four students. An X in the diagram indicates a favorable response to the item by that student and an O indicates an unfavorable response.

| | | ITEMS | |
STUDENTS	A	B	C
1	O	O	O
2	X	O	O
3	X	X	O
4	X	X	X

If the table above represents the actual outcome of giving these three statements to four students, then among these students the items are said to scale. Note that item C is endorsed *only* if item A and item B are both endorsed, and item B is endorsed only if item A is endorsed. A diagrammatic presentation of items and respondents in this form is the basis of Guttman's *scalogram*. If for all subjects the items can be put into the diagonal form shown above—where all of the X's occur together in any row are adjacent—then the items are scaled. The scale positions are given by the order of columns necessary to achieve this grouping. Obviously such a set of items is internally consistent.

On the other hand, suppose that one had an item such as:

D. Students should have a voice in the promotion of faculty. (Agree, Disagree)

Suppose that students gave patterns of responses represented by the following:

	ITEM			
STUDENTS	A	B	C	D
1	0	0	0	0
2	X	X	0	0
3	X	0	0	X
4	X	X	X	X

In this instance the items do not scale, and simple consistency does not seem to be present between items B and D.

An attitude scale constructed according to this principle does not automatically give numerical weights to items; but it does provide an ordinal measurement procedure for attitude measurement, along with a method for achieving as nearly consistent sets of items as possible.

SCALING PROCEDURES AND LEVEL OF MEASUREMENT

How does one determine whether the values obtained by some psychological scaling method are on a ratio, interval, or perhaps ordinal scale? If, truly, these resultant values are on a ratio scale, there should be some *behaviorally* well-defined zero point, which is unique and unchangeable. Thus, for example, the result of Fechnerian psychophysics gives values for R in which amounts of sensation must be in the relation

$$R = K \log(S/L)$$

to the stimulus value in physical units where L is the liminal value. By defining the limen, L, as the physical stimulus intensity that can be detected as present with probability of exactly .5 over independently repeated trials, we define explicitly what we mean by $R = 0$. That is, if the stimulus value S is equal to L, the limen value, then

$$R = K \log (L/L) = K \log (1) = 0.$$

This behavior, defining the limen on such a psychophysical scale, uniquely defines what is meant by the value zero in terms of sensation. We are simply not free to attach the value "zero sensation" to any chosen stimulus. The stimulus getting value $R = 0$ is *behaviorally* defined.

On the other hand, as in any ratio scale, ratios of values are invariant when such values are multiplied by an arbitrary constant. This is true of R, or sensation, values, since if two sensation values are each multiplied by the same constant C, they, nevertheless, refer to the same stimulus intensities:

$$CR_2/CR_1 = \log(S_2/L)/\log(S_1/L).$$

Furthermore, if the stimulus intensities are each multiplied by the same positive constant, they produce sensations in the same ratio as before:

$$\log(CS_2/CL)/\log(CS_1/CL) = \log(S_2/L)/\log(S_1/L) = R_2/R_1.$$

This says that, as in any ratio scale, the size of the unit of measurement, either in terms of stimulus intensity or of sensation, is quite arbitrary.

Consider now the results of another variety of scaling procedure such as Thurstone Scaling by the Law of Comparative Judgment. In this instance, there is really no behaviorally defined zero point. Any stimulus value could just as well be called zero as any other. In practice, one usually takes the zero point to be the mean of the obtained stimulus values and the unit of measurement to be the variance of the difference between stimulus values; but any zero point and unit could be used. One can transform the obtained values by multiplying by any positive constant and adding any constant at all, and these values would predict the same behaviors on the part of the subject. For example, under the usual assumptions made in Thurstone Scaling, if a stimulus A in a Thurstone scale has a value of 1.6 and stimulus B a value of 1, then a subject should report that A exceeds B approximately 77 percent of the time and B exceeds A approximately 23 percent of the time when this pair of stimuli is presented to him. On the other hand, suppose we multiply each of the stimulus values by the constant 10 and add 50 to each to make the values of A and B 66 and 60, respectively. The value of the standard deviation of a difference is now equal to 10, and one would still predict exactly the same proportions of judgments of A over B and B over A for any subject. Thus, Thurstone scaling gives an interval scale of stimulus values that are *behaviorally invariant* when transformed linearly (that is, by multiplication by a positive constant, and addition of any constant).

Finally, suppose that we make up a fairly simple-minded test of some personality characteristic, such as degree of introversion. This test consists of 100 statements to which subjects respond, and the score of any person is simply the number of items to which he responds in an introversive way. Here, there really is no behaviorally defined zero point. One could quite easily define any possible score value to be zero introversion and subtract that score value from each individual's score without altering what these scores actually *mean* in terms of introversive behavior as shown by the test. Furthermore, so long as one preserves the order of magnitude of the scores, one can change the obtained scores in any way he sees fit and still have no reason to say that the new scores predict introversive behaviors that are different from the original scores. Indeed, the scores on such a test really inform one only of the order of magnitude of introversion actually possessed by each individual. The test scales the individuals only at the ordinal level. We lack the rationale for saying anything about the differences in behavior indicated by a score of 50 as opposed to a score of 51. One cannot say that scores of 50 and 51 are behaviorally as different from each other as scores of 10 and 11. Considerably more theory and evidence would have to exist before one would be justified in calling this test measurement at more than the ordinal level.

In short, the scale level and the meaning of the numbers arrived at in psychological measurement depend on the *behaviors* these numbers imply. The scale level can be adjudged from the ways in which these numbers may be transformed and still predict the same behaviors on the part of the subject. One's ability to judge the scale level afforded by the measurement technique depends directly on how much theory and empirical evidence is at one's disposal in measuring the property under study. The ability of the psychologist or any other scientist to measure quantitatively depends on how much he knows or is willing to assume about the connections between the events he observes and the underlying property of interest.

Naturally, the more the numerical values resulting from a particular scaling procedure predict about the behaviors of a subject, the more easily can such scales be validated. Thus, psychophysical scales can sometimes be subjected to quite explicit experimental tests, and the theory that underlies the scales can be examined and modified accordingly. The goodness of a Thurstone scale can be checked by seeing how well the scale values provided actually do reproduce the pair-comparison responses of the subjects. By observing the extent to which new groups of subjects produce the predicted pair comparison judgments, one has further validation. Mental test scores are validated in terms of the differences in some criterion behavior that differences in test scores predict. The more specific and concrete the prediction of behavior the easier is the question of experimental validation.

Most emphatically, this discussion is not meant to imply that somehow ratio scales are good and ordinal scales bad. One must start somewhere in learning to measure, and refined measurement techniques can only be attained if knowledge is first accumulated by means of tentative, and less refined, techniques. In particular, one can study relations between variables measured in a variety of measurement forms. The scale of measurement employed really has little bearing on how one may wish to compare and contrast data qua data. It is only when one wishes to go further and interpret numerical values in terms of the psychological states they represent and behaviors they should predict that one must weigh the evidence and rationale underlying the measurement technique.

OTHER METHODS

It should be obvious that the discussion of measurement and scaling methods given here represents only a small part of the body of existent and potential measurement methods in psychology. Most notably, we have not dealt with situations in which values provided by some physical measuring device are interpreted to be indicators of psychological values. For instance, the psychogalvanic skin response was long taken as a direct measure of emotional arousal. Here, the actual property measured was the electrical conductance of the skin as shown physically by the deflection of a galvanometer. However, for various theoretical and empirical reasons this purely physical measure was taken to represent the psychological condition of emotional arousal. Modern evidence, incidentally, is beginning to cast serious doubts on the simple interpretation of such a direct physical measurement in terms of a psychological state; but in principle, psychological states can be measured by their concommitant physical manifestations. Any number of other direct electrical or other physical measuring techniques have been and are being studied for possible relationships with psychological states or conditions.

Furthermore, although several methods for scaling stimulus objects have been discussed and mental tests designed for scaling persons by their responses to stimuli have been examined, there is a third logical category of measurement operation. Measurement operations exist in which *both* the stimulus objects and the characteristics positions of subjects are simultaneously scaled according to some psychological trait. Recall that in stimulus scaling the task of the subject is to adopt a substantive point of view and to give the direction and extent by which varying stimulus objects appear to differ. In both classical psychophysics and in more modern stimulus scaling methods, the subject or group of subjects is regarded as fixed, and only the stimuli are considered to vary systematically. Any differences in response of different subjects to the same stimuli are treated as statistical error. On the other hand, in mental test methods the test stimuli are regarded as fixed, and individual differences among subjects are the focus of interest. Any difference in the tendency of otherwise equivalent stimuli to evoke differing responses from a subject is written off as statistical error. Thus, for example, if two items on a homogeneous test evoke different responses from the same subject, this is considered to be evidence for unreliability. However, in some instances, the responses of the subjects can be considered to reflect *both* stimulus differences and individual differences. For example, in the scalogram analysis discussed above, not only are attitude items arranged in order by this method but also the respondents by the pattern of items they endorse. The *joint scale* derived from the analysis of such data then pictures not only the differences between stimulus values but also differences between the characteristic positions of individuals. The most extensive work on such joint scaling procedures has been done by C. H. Coombs (1965), and by L. Guttman (1948), particularly in the context of preferential choice and attitude scaling, respectively. Unfortunately, space does not allow a thorough discussion of this topic. The interested student is directed to the sources given above for a look at these relatively recent developments.

On the horizon of developments in psychological measurement may be quantification of psychological states or characteristics by methods from psychopharmacology, biological chemistry, and electrophysiology. The chemistry of the central nervous system is gradually becoming much better understood. Some day intelligence or the feeling of anxiety may be quantified by measurements of amounts of particular chemical substances in the brain. Similarly, measurement of the degree and pattern of electrical activity in the nervous system may eventually lead to direct quantification of psychological states. As theoretical and empirical knowledge grows in all areas of psychological investigation, methods for quantification will undoubtedly grow more numerous and sophisticated.

In summary, then, a method for psychological (as distinct from physical) measurement depends on behaviors of one or more individuals in the presence of one or more stimuli and on some rational procedure for translating those behaviors into numerical values for the stimuli, for the individuals, or for both according to the magnitude or amount of some psychological characteristic. The information in the behavioral data, and hence the information in the final scaled values, depends on what is regarded as fixed in the situation and what is varied. Finally, there must be assumed relations between the behaviors and the psychological magnitudes of the stimuli. These assumed relations may be purely theoretical or purely empirical, although ideally the relations assumed should be grounded both in theory and observation. At the very least, however, the assumed relation between psychological event and behavior should be explicit and reasonable. The assumption of different relations between the unknown psychological quantities and the behaviors one observes will lead to different scaling techniques and to assignment of different values to stimuli or persons.

Although validity and reliability are usually discussed in the context of mental tests, these concepts pervade all of measurement theory. The emphasis placed here upon the explicitly theoretical and experimental underpinnings of any measurement technique is, of course, an argument that measurement should have at least construct validity to justify it. No measurement technique, however, gains wide currency until it stands the test of predictive validity. The lesson to be learned from the development of all of the sciences is that *measurement techniques develop and are refined because they work.* Any measurement procedure must yield *predictive* relations with the other variables and phenomena studied by the scientist. Hence, the goodness of a technique depends not on the elegance of its theory or of its apparatus but on how the results of its application fit into the overall search for relations. Similarly, the reliability of any measurement procedure becomes apparent in the consistency of the numbers it yields and in the degree to which values predict themselves over repeated measurement occasions. Both validity and reliability are ultimately questions of the predictive goodness of the values obtained—the extent to which the values obtained by measurement are related in the right ways to the right things.

EXERCISES AND PROBLEMS

1. Make up an example of a psychological trait that might be measureable by (a) some direct technique, and (b) by an indirect method.

2. Distinguish, in your own words, between *psychophysics* and *psychometrics.*

3. You are called upon to take a test for the U.S. Selective Service System to qualify you for draft exemption. Is this a psychometric test? In what sense?

4. A measure such as heart rate or a rating of leadership potential as measured by an unseen observer may each be a psychometric measure. How do these two measures differ, and how are they similar? Explain in some detail.

5. In standardized tests, the differences among individuals are treated as significant and are considered to reflect differing characteristics of individuals. In psychometrics, differences among individuals are often treated as error. Elaborate on the differences among these two approaches.

6. In a well-known industrial test, an individual is given a score that compares him in rank to all of the individuals who have ever taken the test. Would you say that this was a standardized test? Why?

7. In a Rorschach Ink Blot Test, the individual is often characterized by the internal evidence the test affords. Is this test standardized

when so used? On the other hand, manuals for this test tell relatively how often a standard group gave particular responses. Rare responses are pointed out. Is the test standardized when used in this way? Why?

8. Give an example of a pure speed test. Do not use the one given in the text. How does one recognize a pure speed test?

9. If you were given a pure power test, how would you recognize it?

10. How would you go about assessing the difficulty of a set of items in a power test as referred to a specific set of subjects?

11. Suppose you were given the task of constructing an empirically based test of *honesty* among college students. How would you go about constructing such a test?

12. Some people feel that psychological tests represent an invasion of the privacy of students to whom they are given. Would you say that this charge, if true, applies more to tests that are empirically based or more to those that have a high theoretical basis?

13. Why is it necessary that items on a homogeneous test be correlated, while those of a pure power test need show only minimal correlation?

14. Make up an example of a discriminating item for a test that is to distinguish between serious college students and those who are potential flunkouts. Assume that each criterion group answers the questions candidly.

15. Discuss the concept of validity in all of its various shades of meaning.

16. Compare the theory of test reliability to the theory underlying Thurstone scaling as discussed in Chapter II. What changes are necessary to make one theoretical basis correspond to the other?

17. It can be seen from the theory of test reliability that the following statement is true: If the variability to error is _____ relative to the variability due to true differences, _____ the test will tend to be _____.

18. When a test is said to be valid because it correlates well with tests that presumably measure the same thing, it is said to have _____ validity.

19. When a test is said to be valid because theory dictates that it should measure a particular thing, then it is said to have _____ validity.

20. When a test, regardless of its makeup, predicts the things that it should predict, it is said to have _____ validity.

21. Ordinarily, mental tests can be thought of as providing at most _____ level of measurement.

APPENDIX: NORMAL-CURVE PROBABILITIES AND DENSITIES

z Value	Probability in Interval below z	Density f(x)	z Value	Probability in Interval below z	Density f(x)
0.00	.5000	.3989	0.40	.6554	.3683
0.01	.5040	.3989	0.41	.6591	.3668
0.02	.5080	.3989	0.42	.6628	.3653
0.03	.5120	.3988	0.43	.6664	.3637
0.04	.5160	.3986	0.44	.6700	.3621
0.05	.5199	.3984	0.45	.6736	.3605
0.06	.5239	.3982	0.46	.6772	.3589
0.07	.5279	.3980	0.47	.6808	.3572
0.08	.5319	.3977	0.48	.6844	.3555
0.09	.5359	.3973	0.49	.6879	.3538
0.10	.5398	.3970	0.50	.6915	.3521
0.11	.5438	.3965	0.51	.6950	.3503
0.12	.5478	.3961	0.52	.6985	.3485
0.13	.5517	.3956	0.53	.7019	.3467
0.14	.5557	.3951	0.54	.7054	.3448
0.15	.5596	.3945	0.55	.7088	.3429
0.16	.5636	.3939	0.56	.7123	.3410
0.17	.5675	.3932	0.57	.7157	.3391
0.18	.5714	.3925	0.58	.7190	.3372
0.19	.5753	.3918	0.59	.7224	.3352
0.20	.5793	.3910	0.60	.7257	.3332
0.21	.5832	.3902	0.61	.7291	.3312
0.22	.5871	.3894	0.62	.7324	.3292
0.23	.5910	.3885	0.63	.7357	.3271
0.24	.5948	.3876	0.64	.7389	.3251
0.25	.5987	.3867	0.65	.7422	.3230
0.26	.6026	.3857	0.66	.7454	.3209
0.27	.6064	.3847	0.67	.7486	.3187
0.28	.6103	.3836	0.68	.7517	.3166
0.29	.6141	.3825	0.69	.7549	.3144
0.30	.6179	.3814	0.70	.7580	.3123
0.31	.6217	.3802	0.71	.7611	.3101
0.32	.6255	.3790	0.72	.7642	.3079
0.33	.6293	.3778	0.73	.7673	.3056
0.34	.6331	.3765	0.74	.7704	.3034
0.35	.6368	.3752	0.75	.7734	.3011
0.36	.6406	.3739	0.76	.7764	.2989
0.37	.6443	.3726	0.77	.7794	.2966
0.38	.6480	.3712	0.78	.7823	.2943
0.39	.6517	.3697	0.79	.7852	.2920

z Value	Probability in Interval below z	Density $f(x)$	z Value	Probability in Interval below z	Density $f(x)$
0.80	.7881	.2897	1.30	.9032	.1714
0.81	.7910	.2874	1.31	.9049	.1691
0.82	.7939	.2850	1.32	.9066	.1669
0.83	.7967	.2827	1.33	.9082	.1647
0.84	.7995	.2803	1.34	.9099	.1626
0.85	.8023	.2780	1.35	.9115	.1604
0.86	.8051	.2756	1.36	.9131	.1582
0.87	.8078	.2732	1.37	.9147	.1561
0.88	.8106	.2709	1.38	.9162	.1539
0.89	.8133	.2685	1.39	.9177	.1518
0.90	.8159	.2661	1.40	.9192	.1497
0.91	.8186	.2637	1.41	.9207	.1476
0.92	.8212	.2613	1.42	.9222	.1456
0.93	.8238	.2589	1.43	.9236	.1435
0.94	.8264	.2565	1.44	.9251	.1415
0.95	.8289	.2541	1.45	.9265	.1394
0.96	.8315	.2516	1.46	.9279	.1374
0.97	.8340	.2492	1.47	.9292	.1354
0.98	.8365	.2468	1.48	.9306	.1334
0.99	.8389	.2444	1.49	.9319	.1315
1.00	.8413	.2420	1.50	.9332	.1295
1.01	.8438	.2396	1.51	.9345	.1276
1.02	.8461	.2371	1.52	.9357	.1257
1.03	.8485	.2347	1.53	.9370	.1238
1.04	.8508	.2323	1.54	.9382	.1219
1.05	.8531	.2299	1.55	.9394	.1200
1.06	.8554	.2275	1.56	.9406	.1182
1.07	.8577	.2251	1.57	.9418	.1163
1.08	.8599	.2227	1.58	.9429	.1145
1.09	.8621	.2203	1.59	.9441	.1127
1.10	.8643	.2179	1.60	.9452	.1109
1.11	.8665	.2155	1.61	.9463	.1092
1.12	.8686	.2131	1.62	.9474	.1074
1.13	.8708	.2107	1.63	.9484	.1057
1.14	.8729	.2083	1.64	.9495	.1040
1.15	.8749	.2059	1.65	.9505	.1023
1.16	.8770	.2036	1.66	.9515	.1006
1.17	.8790	.2012	1.67	.9525	.0989
1.18	.8810	.1989	1.68	.9535	.0973
1.19	.8830	.1965	1.69	.9545	.0957
1.20	.8849	.1942	1.70	.9554	.0940
1.21	.8869	.1919	1.71	.9564	.0925
1.22	.8888	.1895	1.72	.9573	.0909
1.23	.8907	.1872	1.73	.9582	.0893
1.24	.8925	.1849	1.74	.9591	.0878
1.25	.8944	.1826	1.75	.9599	.0863
1.26	.8962	.1804	1.76	.9608	.0848
1.27	.8980	.1781	1.77	.9616	.0833
1.28	.8997	.1758	1.78	.9625	.0818
1.29	.9015	.1736	1.79	.9633	.0804

z Value	Probability in Interval below z	Density $f(x)$	z Value	Probability in Interval below z	Density $f(x)$
1.80	.9641	.0790	2.30	.9893	.0283
1.81	.9649	.0775	2.31	.9896	.0277
1.82	.9656	.0761	2.32	.9898	.0270
1.83	.9664	.0748	2.33	.9901	.0264
1.84	.9671	.0734	2.34	.9904	.0258
1.85	.9678	.0721	2.35	.9906	.0252
1.86	.9686	.0707	2.36	.9909	.0246
1.87	.9693	.0694	2.37	.9911	.0241
1.88	.9699	.0681	2.38	.9913	.0235
1.89	.9706	.0669	2.39	.9916	.0229
1.90	.9713	.0656	2.40	.9918	.0224
1.91	.9719	.0644	2.41	.9920	.0219
1.92	.9726	.0632	2.42	.9922	.0213
1.93	.9732	.0620	2.43	.9925	.0208
1.94	.9738	.0608	2.44	.9927	.0203
1.95	.9744	.0596	2.45	.9929	.0198
1.96	.9750	.0584	2.46	.9931	.0194
1.97	.9756	.0573	2.47	.9932	.0189
1.98	.9761	.0562	2.48	.9934	.0184
1.99	.9767	.0551	2.49	.9936	.0180
2.00	.9772	.0540	2.50	.9938	.0175
2.01	.9778	.0529	2.51	.9940	.0171
2.02	.9783	.0519	2.52	.9941	.0167
2.03	.9788	.0508	2.53	.9943	.0163
2.04	.9793	.0498	2.54	.9945	.0158
2.05	.9798	.0488	2.55	.9946	.0154
2.06	.9803	.0478	2.56	.9948	.0151
2.07	.9808	.0468	2.57	.9949	.0147
2.08	.9812	.0459	2.58	.9951	.0143
2.09	.9817	.0449	2.59	.9952	.0139
2.10	.9821	.0440	2.60	.9953	.0136
2.11	.9826	.0431	2.61	.9955	.0132
2.12	.9830	.0422	2.62	.9956	.0129
2.13	.9834	.0413	2.63	.9957	.0126
2.14	.9838	.0404	2.64	.9959	.0122
2.15	.9842	.0395	2.65	.9960	.0119
2.16	.9846	.0387	2.66	.9961	.0116
2.17	.9850	.0379	2.67	.9962	.0113
2.18	.9854	.0371	2.68	.9963	.0110
2.19	.9857	.0363	2.69	.9964	.0107
2.20	.9861	.0355	2.70	.9965	.0104
2.21	.9864	.0347	2.71	.9966	.0101
2.22	.9868	.0339	2.72	.9967	.0099
2.23	.9871	.0332	2.73	.9968	.0096
2.24	.9875	.0325	2.74	.9969	.0093
2.25	.9878	.0317	2.75	.9970	.0091
2.26	.9881	.0310	2.76	.9971	.0088
2.27	.9884	.0303	2.77	.9972	.0086
2.28	.9887	.0297	2.78	.9973	.0084
2.29	.9890	.0290	2.79	.9974	.0081

z Value	Probability in Interval below z	Density f(x)	z Value	Probability in Interval below z	Density f(x)
2.80	.9974	.0079	3.30	.9995	.0017
2.81	.9975	.0077	3.31	.9995	.0017
2.82	.9976	.0075	3.32	.9996	.0016
2.83	.9977	.0073	3.33	.9996	.0016
2.84	.9977	.0071	3.34	.9996	.0015
2.85	.9978	.0069	3.35	.9996	.0015
2.86	.9979	.0067	3.36	.9996	.0014
2.87	.9979	.0065	3.37	.9996	.0014
2.88	.9980	.0063	3.38	.9996	.0013
2.89	.9981	.0061	3.39	.9997	.0013
2.90	.9981	.0060	3.40	.9997	.0012
2.91	.9982	.0058	3.41	.9997	.0012
2.92	.9982	.0056	3.42	.9997	.0012
2.93	.9983	.0055	3.43	.9997	.0011
2.94	.9984	.0053	3.44	.9997	.0011
2.95	.9984	.0051	3.45	.9997	.0010
2.96	.9985	.0050	3.46	.9997	.0010
2.97	.9985	.0048	3.47	.9997	.0010
2.98	.9986	.0047	3.48	.9998	.0009
2.99	.9986	.0046	3.49	.9998	.0009
3.00	.9987	.0044	3.50	.9998	.0009
3.01	.9987	.0043	3.51	.9998	.0008
3.02	.9987	.0042	3.52	.9998	.0008
3.03	.9988	.0040	3.53	.9998	.0008
3.04	.9988	.0039	3.54	.9998	.0008
3.05	.9989	.0038	3.55	.9998	.0007
3.06	.9989	.0037	3.56	.9998	.0007
3.07	.9989	.0036	3.57	.9998	.0007
3.08	.9990	.0035	3.58	.9998	.0007
3.09	.9990	.0034	3.59	.9998	.0006
3.10	.9990	.0033	3.60	.9998	.0006
3.11	.9991	.0032	3.61	.9999	.0006
3.12	.9991	.0031	3.62	.9999	.0006
3.13	.9991	.0030	3.63	.9999	.0006
3.14	.9992	.0029	3.64	.9999	.0005
3.15	.9992	.0028	3.65	.9999	.0005
3.16	.9992	.0027	3.66	.9999	.0005
3.17	.9992	.0026	3.67	.9999	.0005
3.18	.9993	.0025	3.68	.9999	.0005
3.19	.9993	.0025	3.69	.9999	.0004
3.20	.9993	.0024	3.70	.9999	.0004
3.21	.9993	.0023	3.71	.9999	.0004
3.22	.9994	.0022	3.72	.9999	.0004
3.23	.9994	.0022	3.73	.9999	.0004
3.24	.9994	.0021	3.74	.9999	.0004
3.25	.9994	.0020	3.75	.9999	.0004
3.26	.9994	.0020	3.76	.9999	.0003
3.27	.9995	.0019	3.77	.9999	.0003
3.28	.9995	.0018	3.78	.9999	.0003
3.29	.9995	.0018	3.79	.9999	.0003

z Value	Probability in Interval below z	Density $f(x)$	z Value	Probability in Interval below z	Density $f(x)$
3.80	.9999	.0003	4.00	1.0000	.0001
3.81	.9999	.0003	4.05	1.0000	.0001
3.82	.9999	.0003	4.10	1.0000	.0001
3.83	.9999	.0003	4.15	1.0000	.0001
3.84	.9999	.0003	4.20	1.0000	.0001
3.85	.9999	.0002	4.25	1.0000	.0001
3.86	.9999	.0002	4.30	1.0000	.0000
3.87	1.0000	.0002	4.35	1.0000	.0000
3.88	1.0000	.0002	4.40	1.0000	.0000
3.89	1.0000	.0002	4.45	1.0000	.0000
3.90	1.0000	.0002	4.50	1.0000	.0000
3.91	1.0000	.0002	4.55	1.0000	.0000
3.92	1.0000	.0002	4.60	1.0000	.0000
3.93	1.0000	.0002	4.65	1.0000	.0000
3.94	1.0000	.0002	4.70	1.0000	.0000
3.95	1.0000	.0002	4.75	1.0000	.0000
3.96	1.0000	.0002	4.80	1.0000	.0000
3.97	1.0000	.0002	4.85	1.0000	.0000
3.98	1.0000	.0001	4.90	1.0000	.0000
3.99	1.0000	.0001	4.95	1.0000	.0000

Anastasi, Anne. *Differential psychology: Individual and group differences in behavior*, 3rd ed. New York: Macmillan, 1956.

Coombs, C. H. *A theory of data*. New York: Wiley, 1964.

Cronbach, L. J. *Essentials of psychological testing*, 2nd ed. New York: Harper, 1960.

Guilford, J. P. *Psychometric methods*, 2nd ed. New York: McGraw-Hill, 1954.

Guttman, L. The basis for scalogram analysis. In S. A. Stouffer, et al., *Measurement and prediction*. Princeton, N. J.: Princeton University Press, 1950.

Hays, W. L. *Statistics for psychologists*. New York: Holt, 1963.

Johada, Marie, Deutsch, M., and Cook, S. W. *Research methods in social relations*. New York: Dryden, 1951.

Stevens, S. S. On the psychophysical law. *Psychol. Rev.*, 1957, *64*, 153–81.

_____. Problems and methods of psychophysics. *Psychol. Bull.*, 1958, *55*, 177–196.

_____. The quantification of sensation. *Daedalus*, 1959, *88*, 606–621.

Thurstone, L. L. The method of paired comparisons for social values. *J. abnorm. soc. Psychol.*, 1927, *21*, 384–400.

Torgerson, W. S. *Theory and methods of scaling*. New York: Wiley, 1958.

Tyler, Leona E. *The psychology of human differences*. New York: Appleton-Century-Crofts, 1956.

Date Due